Tom Clancy's RAINBOW SIX 3

Prima's Official Strategy Guide

Michael Searle

The Prima Games logo is a registered trademark of Random House, Inc., registered in the United States and other countries. Primagames.com is a registered trademark of Random House, Inc., registered in the United States.

© 2003 by Prima Games. All rights reserved. No part of this book may be reproduced or transmitted in any form or by any means, electronic or mechanical, including photocopying, recording, or by any information storage or retrieval system without written permission from Prima Games. Prima Games is a division of Random House, Inc.

Product Manager: Jill Hinckley
Project Editor: Matt Sumpter
Design & Layout: Graphic Applications Group, Inc.

©2003 Red Storm Entertainment. All Rights Reserved. Rainbow Six, Red Storm, and Red Storm Entertainment are trademarks of Red Storm Entertainment in the U.S. and/or other countries. Red Storm Entertainment, Inc. is a Ubisoft Entertainment company. Ubisoft, the Ubisoft logo, and the soldier icon are trademarks of Ubisoft Entertainment in the U.S. and/or other countries.

All products and characters mentioned in this book are trademarks of their respective companies.

Please be advised that the ESRB rating icons, "EC", "K-A", "E", "T", "M", "AO" and "RP" are copyrighted works and certification marks owned by the Entertainment Software Association and the Entertainment Software Rating Board and may only be used with their permission and authority. Under no circumstances may the rating icons be self-applied or used in connection with any product that has not been rated by the ESRB. For information regarding whether a product has been rated by the ESRB, please call the ESRB at 1-800-771-3772 or visit www.esrb.org. For information regarding licensing issues, please call the ESA at (212) 223-8936. Please note that ESRB ratings only apply to the content of the game itself and does NOT apply to the content of this book.

Important:
Prima Games has made every effort to determine that the information contained in this book is accurate. However, the publisher makes no warranty, either expressed or implied, as to the accuracy, effectiveness, or completeness of the material in this book; nor does the publisher assume liability for damages, either incidental or consequential, that may result from using the information in this book. The publisher cannot provide information regarding game play, hints and strategies, or problems with hardware or software. Questions should be directed to the support numbers provided by the game and device manufacturers in their documentation. Some game tricks require precise timing and may require repeated attempts before the desired result is achieved.

ISBN: 0-7615-4391-0
Library of Congress Catalog Card Number: 2003111493
Printed in the United States of America

03 04 05 06 GG 10 9 8 7 6 5 4 3 2 1

Prima Games
A Division of Random House, Inc.

3000 Lava Ridge Court
Roseville, CA 95661
(800) 733-3000
www.primagames.com

Contents

TERROR STRIKE

All of your missions will be covert and dangerous.

The biggest threat to the world comes from a small group of terrorists. We don't know names. We don't know the ultimate agenda. We don't know how far they're willing to go.

We do know they're very dangerous.

That's where your special commando team of *Rainbow Six 3* agents comes into play. You lead a team of three other special operatives to hamper and thwart global terror in all its ugly manifestations. Hostage situation in the Alps? You infiltrate the village and eliminate the enemy. Bomb set to go off in a commuter tunnel? You deactivate the

Stop the terrorists before too many people get hurt.

explosives and hunt down the perpetrators. When the world's threatened, your job is to put everyone at ease—with a permanent solution.

Dropping out of a motoring helicopter is like punching a time card for your special operatives.

Sixth Sense

By chopper or truck, your team will infiltrate at the weakest point of the defense to have the strongest chance of success.

Your five senses won't be good enough to get you through the terror trials ahead. Not only will you have to be on top of your game—noticing a bit of movement in the shadows or picking out the creak of a floorboard—but you'll have to rely on combat-honed instinct to win the day.

You can get a head start on developing your *Rainbow Six* instincts with a healthy helping of experience. **Basic Training** provides all the basic game strategies, while **Combat Tactics** gets into the intricacies of fighting against savvy terrorists in unfavorable conditions. For those who want to know their M1 from their M4, or how to

Dodging explosions and assaulting impossible positions are par for the course on your missions.

use a smoke grenade to maximum effect, flip over to the weapons details in **Weapons Academy**. Fans of multiplayer battles should turn to the **Xbox Live** section to get the full skinny on team tactics and online secrets.

Or maybe you already have what it takes to identify and eliminate terrorists. Been through some scrapes and came away with just a Band-Aid to show? If you don't think you need strategy pointers, hop on over to the walkthrough and read the ins and outs for each of the game's missions. Guaranteed you'll learn something as each section details enemy positions, terrorist tendencies, alternate scenarios, and the best route to completing each mission.

Be ready for anything in this game.

Like a RAINBOW in the Dark

When things look dark, you bring a ray of hope to people in desperate need. Against the senseless and brutal aggression terror brings to the globe, you combat the evil with your weapons of justice and mercy. No matter the mission, your team will be asked to do the impossible and make it look easy.

Get out of the way if you don't like nail-biting combat scenarios.

BASIC TRAINING

Can you outperform the best? Do you have what it takes to command a secret mission or stay cool while the bullets whiz by your head? *Rainbow Six 3* is all about what you can do in combat, and more importantly, what you and your team can do in combat. Whether you've weathered a war like Patton or it's your first field mission, the following chapter can help you learn or perfect your craft. We'll show you where and how to shoot; you'll have to pull the trigger.

Battle terrorists in kitchens, in the dark, anywhere they try to infiltrate.

Mission Possible

There are 14 missions in *Rainbow Six 3*, though when you boil it all down there are four main mission types. Every mission needs you to keep in mind all facets of your job, but you can focus on a few main things to help you through the mission theme.

Certain missions will require perfect execution or someone on your side will end up dead.

Hostage Rescue

Speed or stealth rescues hostages.

In a hostage situation you need surprise or speed to save the innocent civilians. Take your time or screw up an attack and the terrorists will execute the hostages.

If a terrorist spots you on a hostage rescue, you had better drop him before he warns others.

How does this differ from a regular mission? You may opt from the start to go with suppressed-fire weapons. Relying on stealth and silent killings can get you deep enough into the terrorists' space that it will be too late for them to react when you jump in to save the hostages. If you don't go for stealth, you have to choose speed. That means moving quickly through the terrorist-controlled area, picking off any fleeing terrorists that may try to warn their fellows and rushing the few guards that hold the hostages.

While using speed, it's key that you hit all your targets in a very limited time frame, so you want to pay attention to weapon accuracy and damage potential.

You must shoot precisely when innocent lives are on the line.

You may have to use a little speed if you've got a bomb on a timer.

Bomb Removal

Cut the right wire while deactivating a bomb or pack a spare burn ward in your pocket.

Terrorists like to set bombs. You will be called upon over and over to deactivate these bombs, or die trying. Your whole team has the skill to "demo up" and cut the correct wires, but there are some factors to keep in mind around bombs.

Don't worry about shooting a bomb and having it go off. It won't. However, a nearby terrorist may attempt a suicide move and set it off just to spite you.

The terrorists know you're coming for the bomb, so expect heavy resistance. Only after all the enemies are dead should you shut down the bomb. Even then, always look for a trap, since the terrorists like to stage ambushes around the bomb sites.

Expect heavy resistance around key strategic areas like bomb sites.

Finally, some bombs have timers. You can't be careless while assaulting them. You can, however, pick up the pace and dispense with time-consuming recon if time grows short. Give yourself a chance at least to shut it down.

Stealth

You will have to hide in darkness or good cover spots to avoid the guards in stealth missions.

When your superiors tell you to put away your gun, you're going on a stealth mission. It will involve planting a bug or explosives somewhere without being seen. During a stealth mission, you can't shoot off your weapon and you can't let a guard spot you. You will have to rely on shadows, cover, and knowledge of the terrorists' routes to slip in unseen.

Search-and-Destroy

Pull out the big artillery for search-and-destroy missions.

When you don't have hostages, bombs, or stealth objectives, you can just have fun and pull the trigger. Search-and-destroy missions allow maximum firepower and encourage collateral damage of all sorts. Sometimes, you'll be called upon to chase after a moving target; along the way you'll shoot everything in your path. When you're tired of the pressure of narrowly saving a hostage or snipping the bomb wire seconds before ground zero, search-and-destroy delivers a nice change of pace.

Supermen for Everyone

You and the same three soldiers run through every mission together.

Unlike many other combat-simulation games, *Rainbow Six 3*'s soldiers don't have true stats. Consider yourself and your three teammates the best of the best, the ultimate soldier. You can customize your weapons and equipment, but you will always be the same four guys—Chavez, Price, Loiselle, and Weber. No worries about who you want to be, just grab an M16, grenade launcher, gas mask, and go kick some butt.

Recon First

Recon an area so you don't end up lying on the floor.

As you can imagine, it's better to know what's ahead of you so you can plan accordingly. Scout around an area before you or your team charges in. You may spot a hidden enemy up on a balcony that you wouldn't have noticed otherwise, or recognize a trap before it annihilates your whole squad. Also, you need to know what to expect so you can adopt the best plan of attack, especially when you must attack and give orders simultaneously. The only time your eyes aren't better than your men's is in an area where you can't immediately spot an enemy attacker. In cases like that, let your men recon and they might down the threat before you have to worry about it.

Brain vs. Machine

You should lead your team in combat situations.

In nearly every combat situation, it's better for you to lead the charge or dictate the commands to your squad. If you let the game's A.I. take over and send your team blindly into hot spots, you could lose a member or two even in the simplest of firefights. For example, you may ask your team to run through an open door and position themselves on the right side of the corridor, and they'll do just that. However, where you would scour both directions before proceeding, they may not look at the left side as they move out into the hallway, which means bad news if there's an enemy force there.

Command and Conquer

You can give your squad certain commands, like rescuing hostages or securing an area.

Beyond the point, click, and move that navigates your squad most of the time, you can also cycle through certain commands or set them from the action menu. Press the black button and you'll cycle from regrouping (the team catches up and reforms behind you) to moving (if you've set a waypoint) to covering (the team holds and fans out to lay down cover fire).

When you want more complicated maneuvers, call up the action menu. "Open and clear" will be the most common move, which sends your team through a door prepared for a fight on the other side. "Breach and clear" adds a little more oomph to the "open and clear" command. Your team plants some plastic explosives on the door and charges in after the explosion stuns and slays those inside. "Open, frag and clear" has the team open a door, chuck a grenade in for some house-cleaning, and delay a few seconds for the follow-up. Finally, "open, flash and clear" performs a similar maneuver, but this time your team chucks a flashbang grenade in to shock terrorists who may be holding innocent civilians hostage.

Zulu Delay

Unless it's a clear open shot into a room, you may have to rely on a Zulu command to delay your team while you move into place.

If you want to pause your team before they perform a particularly difficult task, especially to give you time to get into position somewhere else, set them on "Zulu." The team will wait and perform the maneuver only after you hit the white Zulu button. You can execute some deadly tag teams if you time the Zulu action just right.

Caution

Be careful that you don't jump the gun on a Zulu operation. Wait until your readout tells you the team has opened the door or dropped the grenade before initiating your half of the maneuver. Otherwise, you could get caught in the explosion or crossfire.

Weapon X

Practice with all the different weapons to feel out the best one for you.

You have so many weapons to choose from, but get only one primary and one secondary. Since your men don't have stats, the guns will define them. Keep in mind that your men will automatically choose weapons based on your pick (they choose the weapons, not you). If you opt for the UMP with suppressed fire, they'll go quiet as well. If you go all-out with bigger assault weapons, expect them to beef up their arsenal. Same goes for the extra equipment. Try on a gas mask and they pull theirs out of the duffel bags. Copycats.

Mapping It Out

The auto-map gives you information about a room before you set foot inside.

The map is your friend. It also gives you X-ray vision of sorts. The auto-map function shows you all the surrounding corridors and rooms, so you can get an accurate idea of room size, door locations, and possibly enemy positions without even entering the place. While searching for mission objectives, the map can save you hours. Marked with a circular X symbol on the map, you can search for these objectives with the map fully open and it will lead you to the prize like the Yellow Brick Road.

Knock, Knock

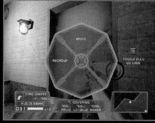

If a door comes up with only the move command, nothing lies on the other side.

Without opening a door, you can tell if an enemy might be behind it or not. Point at the door and call up your squad orders. If you only get a "move" order, it means the door is a dead end and doesn't lead anywhere. Otherwise, it's a live area and may contain terrorists. If you have time, do this around an area and you can pinpoint where the enemy activity will most likely be and make sure your eyes are in that direction at all times. Also, on those rare times when you get lost, this trick can help you find the next leg of your journey.

Two-to-One Advantage

When you take point, you'll dish out damage, but be prepared for return fire.

Normally, your team travels as a group with you at the point. When a confrontation occurs, depending on the terrain and obstacles around, your men will back you up, but you take the brunt of the attacks. That's okay if you like to be in control or are really good at escaping damage; it's not okay if you're low on life or about to enter a trouble spot.

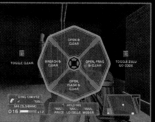

Use the squad commands to work *with* your team.

Why do all the work yourself? You operate even more effectively in tandem with your squad. A simple "move" command can send your other three teammates to a position, while you head to a different location, possibly to flank the enemy or cover two different zones. You could also ask your team to hold in an area and watch your back, while you scout out an unknown section of the map.

Caution

When operating apart from your squad, look out for hitting each other by accident in the crossfire.

Perhaps the most useful function of the tandem is the two-pronged attack. If a room has two entrances, for example, you could send your team to "open and clear" one while you kick in the other. The enemy will be flustered by two different attacks, and you should gain some extra time from the confusion. In areas where there are multiple actions, you can speed things up by having your team do one thing while you do another, such as the team deactivating a bomb while you recon ahead.

Teamwork will wipe out the terrorists or drive them to surrender.

Smoking Can Kill

With thermal vision you can see right through a smoke grenade as if it weren't there.

Want to turn invisible? Throw a smoke grenade into a populated area, then switch to your thermal vision. While the enemy terrorists scurry about trying to escape the smoke, nothing changes for you since thermal operates on body heat. You can even walk all the way up to the site of the billowing smoke to get a better angle. Just remember that the smoke dissipates after about a minute, so make quick work of your opposition.

Back to the Wall

Always aim your gun into new areas by hugging walls with your back. This sets you up against new threats better.

Don't expose yourself to unnecessary fire. A frequent mistake by beginners is to charge into a new area to see what's there. Granted, if you're willing to restart the mission over and over, you can learn the lay of the land that way, but it'll be painful. A safer course might be a plan like this: While entering rooms, rounding corners, and descending stairwells, you always want your gun facing the new area. By hugging walls with your back, you gain cover and maintain position on your eventual enemies.

Experiment to the Max

Whether in the depths of a dungeon or sneaking up on a guard, try out new tactics and moves to master your profession.

Experiment with your weapons and team configurations until you like what you see. Like how your team reacts during a flashbang sequence? Load up on more flashbang grenades and use them even when hostages aren't involved. Find your tactics lean toward the stealthy? Arm yourself with suppressed-weapons and become silent commandos. The only way to become the ultimate commando team is to learn your strengths and weaknesses, and don't let the latter ever surface.

Of course, saving often prevents lots of unnecessary death. Each veteran mission will give you the option to save once or twice (depending on the level's difficulty) at any point on the map. Try to save after you've completed objectives (particularly a mission's second objective) so you don't have to wade through as many bad guys when your restart.

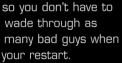

If you want to make it all the way to the end, you'll have to best each mission objective.

WEAPONS ACADEMY

The gun defines the soldier, or at least, helps define how much damage he's going to do against the enemy. Armed with a G3A3, you'll cut through terrorists like a machete through butter.

But what makes the best weapon? It's a combination of range, damage, accuracy, and certain specialties like suppressed fire. When choosing the perfect weapon, forget about caliber or "range". The damage stat explains how lethal it really is, not the caliber numbers, and all weapons of the same type have a similar range number; it's the scope that indicates how far you can really shoot with any precision. Accuracy is vital on missions where you fight a lot of enemies simultaneously, or ones that call for very difficult shots to be made. Finally, check a weapon's ammo capacity to gauge how long a weapon can last on a mission, and choose suppressed-fire weapons on missions where stealth is paramount.

Now let's examine all the weapons and equipment by category. From the top dog to the plain ol' dog, we'll rate each weapon and clue you in on which missions it might be appropriate to carry it along.

Assault Rifles

The bread-and-butter weapons on your campaign, these high-powered rifles can work both outdoors and indoors. Most have a decent range to focus on those faraway tangos in the wilderness and damage scores that will punch through most targets with a single burst. The two best weapons in the game are both assault rifles, ranked at number one and number two right here.

1. G3A3

What's not to like about this beast? It's one of only three weapons with a 49 range score, and its 87 damage easily beats out all other assault rifles and only falls short of five other bulkier weapons. At a 65 accuracy and 3.5x zoom, you are not missing much unless your eyesight's a little blurry to begin with. If it has any weakness

at all, it's the 20-round clips; you might run out of ammo on really long missions, but only if you're careless.

2. M16A2

You could argue that the M16A2 beats out the G3A3. It comes up short on range, but bests the G3A3 on ammo capacity with 30-round clips. Accuracy ranks slightly higher at 74 to the G3A3's 65, but its damage lands more than 20 points lower at 66. Since damage may be the key statistic—the enemy has to stay down when hit or you won't live to get a second shot—the M16A2 earns the runner-up spot instead.

3. L85A1

An all-around solid weapon, the L85A1 has no weaknesses; it's just not as outstanding as the two weapons above it. A 58 damage score clocks in mid-range, while a 63 accuracy puts it above average for assault rifles. It pushes up to number three on the list because of its 3.5x scope. Being able to snipe at range, even down long corridors, can make or break you on certain missions.

4. GALIL ARM

Where the norm on assault rifles remains 30-round clips, the GALIL impresses with a 100-round clip. Sure, it only comes with four drums to slap in, but that's still more ammo than most guns.

he fact that you don't have to reload in the middle of a
ght pushes it up to the fourth spot. It gets big kudos
or eliminating that feeling of frustration when you come
p dry against the last enemy before the objective point.

5. AUG

Much like the
L85A1, the AUG
does just about
everything well. With
stats slightly below
the L85A1, the AUG
drops down to the
middle of the pack.
It's the last assault
rifle with a 3.5x

cope, so tread carefully if you pick any rifle below it
or an outdoor mission.

6. AK-47

More people have
probably heard of this
Russian-based weapon
than any other on the
list. Why? It's
considered a super-
reliable rifle, and when
you look at its stats
you can understand
the thought. A 60

damage and 71 accuracy look great, until you spot the
meager 1.5x scope, the worst in the game. If not for
that fact, the AK-47 would have cracked the top three.

7. FAMAS G2

This funky-shaped
rifle gets the job
done. With a 39
range, 56 damage,
and 60 accuracy,
you can't really
complain about
much, other than its
2x scope. All the
assault rifles are

good, just some are better than others.

8. G36C

Don't be fooled by
the similar name to
our numero uno
assault rifle. The
G36C can't touch
the G3A3, dropping
off in range, nearly
30 points short in
damage, a few in
accuracy, and only a

2x scope. The only reason to take the G36C is that
it's better than the last two on the list.

9. TAR-21

If you want to
challenge your skills,
equip the TAR-21
over, say, the
M16A2. Not that it's
a bad weapon by any
stretch of the imagi-
nation, it just doesn't
have the raw stat
power of the higher-

ranked assault rifles. Variety is the spice of life, though,
so try it out on a mission and see what you think.

10. M4

What could dash you
to the bottom of the
assault rifle list? How
about a meager 49
accuracy? You can't
afford to shoot blanks
when you're fighting
five terrorists at once,
and the M4 does a
good imitation of a

dumbed-down movie prop. If you're really considering the
M4, you may want to check out one of the other
categories instead.

Shotguns

It's point-blank or nothing. Shotguns can deliver a giant blast of damage or they can spatter a bunch of pellets as harmless as confetti. Basically, it comes down to this—if you know all your fighting will be in tight, grab a shotgun for maximum impact.

1. M1

Hey, those "M" designated weapons have a good rep, except for that M4 loser above. The M1 might prove less than stellar at anything more than a range of 8, but hey, 100 damage is good. The sheer kickback on a damaged foe makes the shotgun worth taking every once in a while. The M1 beats out its only other competition in this category with a 34 ammo capacity.

2. USAS-12

A shotgun is a shotgun for the most part. The stats for the USAS are the same as the M1, other than the reload factor. Shotguns in general are *slow* in the reloading department, so choose the one that speeds up the process—which isn't this one.

Submachine Guns

When an assault rifle is too bulky and a pistol too wimpy, look to the medium-sized submachine guns. The majority of them also provide suppressed fire, so you can trigger semi-automatic *silent* attacks. How cool is that? But there's more. The smaller, lightweight weapons move quicker in combat and present a smaller target to those would-be enemy sharpshooters.

1. UMP

Because they have a silencer on them, most suppressed-fire weapons deal significantly less damage. Not the UMP. Despite its suppressed fire rating, it manages to clock in at the highest damage for a submachine gun. Since the submachine guns' weakness in general would be raw killing power, the higher damage potential helps big time.

2. MP5A4

A worthy runner-up to the UMP, the MP5A4 doesn't shoot quiet but does shoot hard. The 21 damage score clocks in second on the submachine gun list, and the 44 accuracy score and 3.5x scope cement it at the number two slot.

3. SR-2

The only other submachine gun to reach the 20-point or better damage score, the SR-2 suffers in accuracy with a 26 rating. It redeems itself a little with a 12 range and decent 2x scope. Oddly enough, it can also be used as a backup weapon.

4. MP5SD5

Another cool silenced submachine gun, the MP5 doesn't carry its weight when it comes to punch power. With an 8 damage rating, some of its hits equate to paintball stings. To crack the upper half of the submachine gun list, it counters with a 47 accuracy and 3.5x scope.

5. P90

Your teammates like to employ the P90 from time to time. It's a habit you'd like to break them of. Not because it's a bad weapon, it's just not extra-special. Good scores like a 14 range, 17 damage, and 39 accuracy give it a home in the middle.

6. TMP

At least it's got a 46 accuracy. Other than that, the TMP would be better off as scrap metal melted into mortar shells or something.

7. MAC 11/9

If you thought the TMP was bad, you don't even want to look at the MAC 11/9 stats. An 8 damage and 27 accuracy puts it in the hall of shame. When out of ammo, just throw it at the enemy; it may hurt them more.

Machine Guns

Powerful weapons if you can manhandle them around. When you know you have a lot of killing to do, and don't care about the racket a million bullets kicks up, look no further than these big guns. Only two weapons fit into this category, but they carry enough weight to fill several slots on the other weapon charts.

1. M60E4

Face it, you only want the machine gun if you can create mayhem. That said, would you rather have a gun that deals 100 damage or one that deals 55? We can't drive 55 either, so strap on the M60E4 for those forays into enemy territory. Just don't expect to hide with this thing.

2. M249

We already know it deals about half the damage as its M60 cousin. Other than that, it's pretty good. It has a slightly better accuracy at 52, 200-round clips of ammo compared to 100-round clips, and a 3.5x scope. Not bad for the runner-up.

Sniper Rifles

These rifles don't work well indoors. Since *RAINBOW Six 3* is filled with indoor missions, you won't find the sniper rifle useful often. If you know a mission takes place completely outside—none do in *RAINBOW Six 3*—or are willing to use the sniper rifle on the outdoor parts and switch to your backup weapon for the closer combat, then the super-range of the assassin's favorite weapon makes sense.

1. M82A1

Talk about maxing out. The M82A1 ranks 100 in range, 100 in damage, 89 in accuracy, and carries a 10x scope. If this were in an assault rifle package with a better reload, you'd be looking at the gun of the century. As it turns out, you have to be careful when you can use it and when you might be thrown into a compromising situation if an enemy suddenly shows up in breathing distance.

2. PSG-1

The PSG-1 settles into the second-place spot solely on the fact that it has half the range as big number one. All its other stats—98 damage, 83 accuracy, 10x scope—nip competently at the heels of the M82A1.

3. AW COVERT

The trick of a suppressed-fire weapon at huge range just wasn't enough to break free of the cellar. Yes, it's great to zing bad guys from across the map and have no one notice. However, it's not so great to shoot at a range of 8 and hit for one-fifth of the other sniper rifles' damage.

Secondary Weapons

Just like the title implies, these are your backup weapons, so they aren't as good as your main ones. Rather than look for raw firepower, the secondary weapon should serve a special need, whether it be an area-effect attack or a nonlethal alternative.

1. M203 HE

While our primary weapon picks off one or two guys at a time, you can switch to the high-explosive version of the grenade launcher to clear a whole room or strike a hard-to-reach cover spot.

2. M203 RP

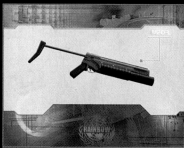

You could argue the phosphorous version of the grenade launcher kills just as effectively as the HE variant, but the high-explosive M203 has a better blast radius.

3. D.EAGLE

The best pistol of the bunch, this .50 caliber special comes with an impressive 70 damage score, better than a lot of rifles. It just doesn't have the range of a primary weapon.

4. MK23

Sometimes you just want to sneak up and whack someone without a loud bang to announce your position. Carry along the MK23 for just this occasion.

5. 92FS

In the same vein as the MK23, the 92FS fires suppressed bullets, but doesn't quite stack up to its predecessor in range or damage.

6. M2O3 CS

For a nonlethal option, try the grenade launcher with tear gas canisters. Against enemies without gas masks, it's a great way to clear out a defensive position.

7. SR-2

It didn't quite make the grade as a primary weapon, but it's not too bad as a secondary weapon with some punch. It's not specialized like many of the guns above it on the list, so it slips down a little.

8. USP

It's got okay stats with a 10 range, 20 damage, and 32 accuracy. By why do you need that in a backup piece?

9. M2O3 SMOKE

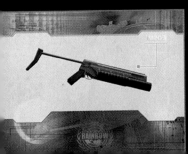

The weakest of the grenade launchers shouldn't really be an option. If you want smoke grenades, take them in the third or fourth equipment slot. You don't want to waste your secondary weapon pick.

10. MAC 11/9

Ah yes, the MAC 11/9. It doubles as a primary and secondary weapon, and that's its only claim to fame. Leave it in the drawer at home.

Equipment

Your third and fourth slots hold general equipment. Here you can load up on grenades, add a breaching charge to your arsenal for those annoying doors, or specialize with a claymore mine to blow someone up from a building away.

1. Flashbang Grenade

Many of your missions will involve hostage rescue, and you can't exactly lob a frag into the room and hope the innocents don't get hit. The flashbang works remarkably well on stunning terrorists and giving you the edge.

2. Breaching Charge

When you need to rush into a room and know the terrorists are waiting on the other side, what better distraction than to blow the door wide open? You can disable enemies with the explosion, and you'll certainly stun them enough to fire first.

3. Frag Grenade

You can never have enough damage-spewing grenades. The frag can down multiple targets and can be chucked into difficult-to-shoot areas to remove resistance.

4. M34 WP Grenade

Another damage grenade, this one incinerates targets rather than fill them full of shrapnel. A smaller radius than the frag, though it does cough up some red smoke for cover.

5. Tear Gas Grenade

When you want to drive enemies crying and choking from an area, the tear gas grenade makes for a good option. Just don't forget your gas mask or you may fall victim to your own scheme.

6. Smoke Grenade

Combined with thermal vision, the smoke grenade can effectively conceal you and set up a kill shot. Because it's not lethal, given the option, you usually want something with more kick.

7. Gas Mask

When you need it, this shoots up to number one on the list—otherwise, you're dead, right? Most missions have no need for a gas mask, so it would just take up space.

8. Remote Charge

One block of C-4 plastic explosive sounds good. Plus, you can detonate it with a remote. You just don't have as much use for it as the breaching charge, which allows you to charge in right away and blast the enemy without delay.

9. Claymore Mine

As with the remote charge, the claymore mine could come in handy if you want to set a trap for a guard and not be seen. Most of the time, however, the straight-forward approach works much better.

Primary Weapons

Weapon	Type	Caliber	Range	Damage	Accuracy	Zoom	Capacity	Suppressed
K-47	Assault Rifle	7.62mm	39	60	71	1.5x	30	No
JG	Assault Rifle	5.56mm	39	57	59	3.5x	30	No
W COVERT	Sniper Rifle	7.62mm	8	20	83	10x	10	Yes
AMAS G2	Assault Rifle	5.56mm	39	56	60	2x	30	No
36C	Assault Rifle	5.56mm	39	56	59	2x	30	No
3A3	Assault Rifle	7.62mm	49	87	65	3.5x	20	No
ALIL ARM	Assault Rifle	5.56mm	39	60	71	1.5x	100	No
35A1	Assault Rifle	5.56mm	39	58	63	3.5x	30	No
1	Shotgun	12g	8	100	1	1.5x	34	No
16A2	Assault Rifle	5.56mm	39	66	74	3.5x	30	No
249	Machine Gun	5.56mm	39	55	52	3.5x	200	No
4	Assault Rifle	5.56mm	39	56	49	2x	30	No
60E4	Machine Gun	7.62mm	49	100	47	1.5x	100	No
82A1	Sniper Rifle	.50cal	100	100	89	10x	10	No
AC 11/9	Submachine Gun	9mm	7	8	27	1.5x	32	Yes
P5A4	Submachine Gun	9mm	11	21	44	3.5x	30	No
P5SD5	Submachine Gun	9mm	7	8	47	3.5x	30	Yes
90	Submachine Gun	5.7mm	14	17	39	2x	50	No
5G-1	Sniper Rifle	7.62mm	49	98	83	10x	10	No
R-2	Submachine Gun	9mm	12	20	26	2x	20	No
AR-21	Assault Rifle	5.56mm	39	52	57	2x	30	No
MP	Submachine Gun	9mm	7	8	46	1.5x	30	Yes
MP	Submachine Gun	.45cal	10	26	43	2x	25	Yes
5AS-12	Shotgun	12g	8	100	1	1.5x	2	No

Secondary Weapons

Weapon	Type	Caliber	Range	Damage	Accuracy	Zoom	Capacity	Suppressed
2FS	Pistol	9mm	7	12	42	1.5x	15	Yes
.EAGLE	Pistol	.50cal	20	70	36	1.5x	7	No
203 CS	Grenade Launcher	40mm	—	—	—	—	4	No
203 HE	Grenade Launcher	40mm	—	—	—	—	4	No
203 RP	Grenade Launcher	40mm	—	—	—	—	4	No
203 SMOKE	Grenade Launcher	40mm	—	—	—	—	4	No
AC 11/9	Submachine Gun	9mm	7	8	27	1.5x	16	No
K23	Pistol	.45cal	8	19	42	1.5x	12	Yes
R-2	Submachine Gun	9mm	12	20	35	1.5x	20	No
5P	Pistol	.40cal	10	20	32	1.5x	13	No

Equipment

Name	Purpose
Breaching Charge	Blows open doors for rapid entry
Claymore Mine	Remotely detonated anti-personnel mine
Flashbang Grenade	Stun observers without injuring potential civilians in the area
Frag Grenade	Damage targets in blast radius
Gas Mask	Protection against toxic gasses
M34 WP Grenade	Incinerates targets in the area with white phosphorus
Remote Charge	1 kilogram block of C-4 plastic explosive with an attached radio detonator
Smoke Grenade	Obscure enemy vision in an area
Tear Gas Grenade	Obscures vision and injures targets without gas masks

COMBAT TACTICS

Without a plan, a single determined enemy can destroy your team.

Pop quiz: Which has a greater range, the M16A2 or the M82A1? If you answered the M16, head back to "Basic Training" class in chapter two. If you went with the sniper rifle, maybe you've graduated from the simple tactics and want some more in-depth breakdowns on certain game situations. From door assaults to setting up crossfires to seeing in the dark, this chapter covers it all—oh yeah, it covers "covering" too.

Door Assault

You must pass through this closed door.

Opening a door seems like such a simple matter. Twist the handle and push the door in, right? Yes, and then taste some lead as the enemy retaliates.

You have to be prepared for the worst at each door. It's best to consider that each unknown door has an enemy or more behind it. So how do you attack such a door?

Check your map at the doorway to see which way to face.

Approach the door and get up as close as you can. You might get lucky and hear footsteps on the other side. A tip like that will save your bacon. You can also try and avoid a fight if you hear the steps receding.

Let's assume you hear zilch (which will be most of the time, since your enemies like to stand quietly and wait for a visual cue to start their attack). While standing next to the door, study your map and glean any information you can from it. Does it look like there's a wall to your left and an open expanse to your right? Play the odds and charge in with your attention focused to the right. If you can peek to your left, it only makes sense to do so and spare yourself a sneak attack if the enemy happens to be there.

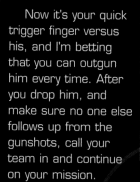

Attack as if an enemy is there.

In our case, a corridor slips off to the right and it doesn't look like there's much to the left. Odds are your enemy would be to the right if he's there at all.

Open the door and sidestep into the corridor with your attention on the right side. Sure enough, you've got an enemy right there lining you up.

Shoot accurately or you'll take a face full of lead.

Now it's your quick trigger finger versus his, and I'm betting that you can outgun him every time. After you drop him, and make sure no one else follows up from the gunshots, call your team in and continue on your mission.

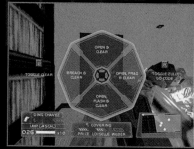

Call your team in when it's safe.

Open, Flash and Clear

Give the "flash and clear" order.

All your team maneuvers operate similarly. You give the order to clear, flash, frag or breach depending on the circumstances. If you don't want to waste equipment, a simple "open and clear" command will do.

Fragging and breaching are for when you want to inflict damage on the terrorists on the other side. Clearing with a flashbang grenade you save for hostage-takers.

Stay back so you don't get flashed.

Approach the door and give the "open, flash and clear" order. If you want it on Zulu—where there's a delay so you can get in position elsewhere—hold the right trigger down before you give the order.

When your men open the door, glance away briefly. You don't want to stare into the flash or you'll lose the advantage it's supposed to give you. Charge into the room after your men. They don't always clear as well as you'd like, so you may need

Charge into the room to help protect your men.

to save one of them from getting pelted by the enemy.

Force the terrorists to surrender or die so you can save the hostage.

Shoot at all terrorists, with an emphasis on the ones with guns pointed at the hostages. Put enough pressure on them and they'll instantly surrender. Otherwise, use short, controlled bursts to keep your fire away from the civilians and into the heads of the terrorists. There is only one acceptable outcome: The hostage goes home without any holes.

Flanking

Shooting from one position can work, but shooting from two different positions is twice as effective. If you can catch the enemy in a crossfire, they won't know what hit them. During the confusion, you will mow them down as they try to decide who to go after.

The enemy position looks tough.

When attacking a difficult enemy position, analyze if there is more than one avenue of attack. If there is, use it. Send your men to one of the strategic spots (maybe through one door) and you head for the second one (maybe another door).

Move your men in one direction.

You head in the other direction.

Attack simultaneously and drive the terrorists to panic. They may not know what direction to turn, so as they swing to attack your men, you cut them down from the side (and vice versa, as your men protect you). By flanking them, you set up a nice crossfire to catch them with the most hits.

You hope to catch the enemy between your arcs of fire.

Do your job and the enemy won't stand a chance.

The battle should go much faster than if you had attacked from a single point. Sometimes, fights like that can go on a long while as you trade shots back and forth. Inevitably, you take damage from a gunfight like that, so look to work together as a team to cut down on unnecessary harm.

Super Vision

Don't run around with your normal peepers. On nighttime missions especially, you need the use of your special visions. Night vision can brighten the darkness into daylight conditions, and you can certainly notice movement better with the brighter whites against the

Shadowy corners can be hard to see into sometimes.

green. Even inside buildings, you may want to switch to night vision to keep things crisp and 100 percent in focus.

Night vision illuminates things a bit.

Human bodies glow through the magic of thermal vision.

In combat, though, thermal vision can't be beat. As long you don't have to navigate through too many obstacles, thermal will pinpoint enemies like a torch in the dark. You can even see heat signatures through barricades and on the other side of locked doors. With so many pressure situations where every shot counts, how can you give up this advantage?

Cover Me

Next up on your agenda is to storm a shipyard guarded by a slew of enemies. At the front of the yard, there's a chokepoint between two stacks of crates that puts you at serious risk—three or four enemy guns are trained in that one area. Yet you need to get through.

Without help, the task of storming the shipyard looks impossible.

Send your team to an elevated point for a superior firing angle.

First, clear out the initial area. Survey the locale and pick out a good cover area. In this case, your team can climb the crates in the yard and cover your back from a superior elevation that overlooks the whole place.

Once they're in position, it's like you've set a trap for anyone who messes with you. As you sprint into the area, the enemies will pop up and your team will identify and eliminate. On your own, you would have to fight five-to-one odds. Not with your team up there, though.

Attack the area on your own.

You can't account for everyone yourself.

Your team kills three of the five enemies, leaving you to mop up the remaining two. The only way to survive dangerous situations is to work together. The cover command can serve as excellent defense in the right circumstances.

In the right place at the right time, your team saves your hide.

You're ready for the real world now. Go score up some weapons and report to your commander for your first briefing. Pretty soon you'll be showing the instructors how things are really done.

Work together as a formidable team and you can beat any mission.

Even familiar maps will be different in multiplayer.

Commanding a squad has its merits, but imagine if you could play through these missions with a few friends or against hordes of raving-lunatic humans. Well, you can. The multiplayer aspect of *RAINBOW Six 3* allows you to enjoy your favorite maps all over again from an entirely different spin. Or maybe not entirely different—you still have to survive.

Multiplayer Madness

So you battled your way through all 14 single-player missions? Time to forget everything you know. Solo and multiplayer are like night and day. Think about it. You pit your mind against other humans in multiplayer, not an A.I., and many of the

Human opponents will be a welcome challenge online.

strategies you applied to a four-man team go out the window when each member of that team can act independently. The following are some fundamental differences.

No Breathers

In single-player mode you can play methodically. Without a clock or someone screaming for help in your ear, you can leisurely recon the area, set up your battle plan and then call the shots when the time is right. It's a different story in multiplayer.

Don't stop moving if you can help it. A moving target makes it difficult or impossible for the enemy to sight you. Against a group of enemies, circle and flank them as you fire.

Don't slow down in multiplayer or you're a target to a lot of guns.

Dancing around increases your odds of living and can set you up for a better angle on any number of enemies.

In cases where you're assaulting an enemy position or there's a target guarded by the enemy, single-player tactics might apply. If you have time, you can set up a long-range shot to minimize the risk. Maneuvers like "breach and clear" can prove effective given time to coordinate.

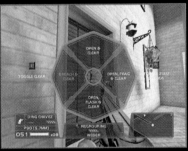

You can still pull off special maneuvers against human opponents if you've got a little extra time.

Lock and Reload

Depending on the size of the battle, you may want to stock up on a weapon with some shells behind it. In longer fights, take the M16A2 over the G3A3 because of its 30-round clips. Throw the suppressed-fire weapons out the window. Stealth is

Guns like the M60E4 will keep you in the fight for a long while.

seldom an option, and the damage potential you sacrifice for such weapons won't be worth it. Unlike the single-player missions, the sniper rifles can be effective if you're designated as a sniper on your team or want to guard a single location with a good view.

If you like to wait for enemies to come to you, the sniper rifle can work on the bigger maps.

The grenade launcher should be your backup weapon. Especially in a game with lots of potential targets, a fragmentation grenade can do in one explosion what a burst of bullets could not. Keep in mind that you can lob grenades down stairwells, over balconies, even bank them around corners in an office. There really is no downside except, maybe, if you get shot in the act of tossing one.

Room for Improvement

You had better know where every toilet on the map is, or at least where each closed door, stairwell, and spawn point is. Where can you find cover under fire? What's the most strategic ambush point? If you don't know it, you can bet your opponent will and make you pay for that mistake.

Know where the hot spots are on your map.

Heard of camping? It's not toasting marshmallows around the fire and telling ghost stories. It's sitting on the best map spots. For example, on the Island Estate map, players might stake out the various balconies to get much better shots on the unfortunates below. You need to

People will tend to camp at key strategic "chokepoints" that you will have to pass through if you want to enjoy another section of the map.

know the favorite camping spots so you can prevent others from gaining them or—join the crowd—and exploit them yourself.

As you play, study all the insertion points. Once you figure them out, you can immediately take off toward your objective without wasting time with the map. When you blow up an enemy, you'll also have an idea of which direction the next one might be coming from. Knowledge of the spawn points can help you plan better attack strategies and give you a "sixth sense," as you can sometimes anticipate the enemy's movement.

Voices in Your Head

In single player, you are the only voice. You tell your teammates what to do, and they do it. It may not be the same in multiplayer unless you're an excellent team leader. Most likely, your teammates

Talk with your allies before diving into combat.

will want to have a say in the battle plan. You need to communicate effectively with them, or you'll be like a lost deer during open season. Appoint one person the leader, and if you get into a disagreement, resolve it quickly, or the enemy will end it for you.

As leader, you plan out the attack for your squad.

Mission Maps

You've played through the single-player missions, so you know each map has a distinct look. What are the best strategies on each one? Where is the prime real estate? Here's a quick look at some of the best spots in the *RAINBOW Six 3* maps.

Alpine Village

The streets of the alpine village will keep you in shape.

The streets are a lot of fun for runnin' and gunnin'. Look for campers at strategic street corners and at the alleyway in front of the church. The church can be the final battleground for one team or the other.

Mountain Highway

You don't have much room out in the tunnel, so expect more people to gravitate to the garage and office areas. The corner office and security room offer great locations to shoot at those outside and jump right back into the fray if shots are fired inside.

The tunnel can prove cramped quarters with lots of people.

Oil Refinery

This maze of walkways and small rooms can be a blast, since you have access to so many different areas and it's not so linear. Watch out for chokepoints like the second bomb room, which can defend the corridor to the second half of the installation rather easily.

The sprawling oil refinery leads to many interesting battle spots.

Island Estate

The balconies will be hot spots, especially the one looking down on the outside steps and the one giving you access to the inner courtyard. If you want a battle among house furniture, this is the map for you.

Beware balconies and unwelcome assassins hiding in them.

Shipyard

Crates, crates, and more crates. Fighting through the maze of crates can prove a challenge, as will defending the large warehouse area. To hold the warehouse, you want several men positioned up on the roof to clear the walkways and hit the enemies worming along the ground floor.

Ladders and the top of crates make for great sniper spots.

Crespo Foundation

The battle for dominance in the offices of the Crespo Foundation will be who can master the stairs. With four floors to navigate, you can control the flow if you can lock a team on a single level.

Hold the stairs to prevent your team from getting overrun.

Old City

Teams will tend to congregate in the building where the informer was held in single-player mode or in the second building, which can serve as a chokepoint to prevent teams from reaching either side of the map. You can have some intense fights throughout the courtyards.

Don't get caught out in the streets without backup.

Alcatraz

Who doesn't want to play in one of the most famous prisons? The sewers can get predictable if you run around in circles, but the upper prison levels make for great multiplayer action. The shower and cellblock in particular spawn brutal fights.

The showers will probably be a bloodbath in multiplayer.

Import/Export

You can get into some struggles around the big loft, but it's not till you run around the truck yard and adjoining warehouse that action heats up. This is one map where you can get away with the sniper rifle if you want to lay low in the truck yard and wait for prey.

The first building offers narrow hallways where grenades seem twice as good.

Penthouse

A very small map that inspires bloody combat. With glass floors and a couple of big spaces like the living room/kitchen area and rooftop, there's really no place to hide. The shotgun works wonders on this map.

You can spot enemies through glass ceilings and doors.

RAINBOW SIX 3

Meat Packing Plant

Hope you're not a vegetarian or you might want to skip this map. The first hostage room can be a trouble spot, since it surveys the room in front of it through its small horizontal window and can successfully defend access to the rest of the facility.

Who would have thought that a cow carcass could provide adequate cover?

Garage

Fights ensue in the showroom all the time, while the tunnel maze below can breed some standoffs. Grenades are a must; they can clear out chunks of resistance when they go off. No one can escape a shrapnel blast in a tight tunnel.

The showroom will showoff some great fights.

Parade

The building between the alleys and the parade float can control tempo, so watch for enemies in those rooms and stairwells. Most likely, the hotel will generate the most action with its multiple levels and outdoors access.

Tread carefully in the alleys with potential snipers on the rooftops above.

Airport

Prepare to think differently inside the airport where it's close combat or out on the tarmac where range plays a factor. The parking lot between the airport and the hangar can serve as a buffer zone between two teams on opposite sides of the map.

While inside the airport you must be on your toes for the enemy who could be around the next corner.

Multiplayer Only Maps

Some RAINBOW Six 3 maps are designed specifically fc multiplayer setups. They're smaller than the mission maps, but strategically created for fast-paced action an fun battlefields. Here are the maps you can load up if you want a different terrain look.

Airport 1

A tight map with lots of corridors that appeals to close-combat freaks. For larger firefights, head to the airport hangar and slug it out between the planes.

Airport 2

Where the first airport map has the indoor real estate, the second airport map gives you the outside perimeter. You can weave through alleys and up fire escapes, but when you want to

slow down and engage in a firefight or two, there's no better place than the parking lot.

City Street Large

It's got an Old West feel—one dusty courtyard for shootouts with lots of building facades to set up ambushes. If the action up top doesn't grab you, head below to the maze of under-ground passages that give you double the gunslinging pleasure.

Run around the back alleyways of the import-export mission map. As you race past strings of hanging clothes, you can air out enemies. Aim for the upper levels so you can gain the elevation advantage on your opponents and watch out for the exploding barrels.

Old City

If you like the golden sunlight-strewn streets from the mission map, you get a new look with the multiplayer version. Wind through the alleys and through all the neighboring apartments. Beware of the hanging sheets that block your view from hidden players.

Peaks

Take the top of the hill in this snow-covered battlefield if you can. Your team can assault downhill a lot easier than climbing up the steep paths. Note that the various lampposts illuminate the local areas and make them difficult to hide in.

Presidio

Most of the map locks players in a struggle through the central building. With ladders all over the place and sandbags strategically sprinkled for protection, big battles can take a

from different doors.

Training

The same training grounds that tutors agents before they let loose in the regular missions serves as an obstacle course in multiplayer. With several rooftops to seize, barricades to navigate and small buildings to recon, this map has ample possibilities.

Warehouse

Another nighttime battlefield, you may not notice the moonlight since you'll be inside the giant warehouse most of the time. With catwalks all over the place and crates to duck behind, seizing the warehouse presents quite a challenge. You will need to command each level—even the rooftop—to succeed.

MISSION 1: ALPINE VILLAGE

Terrorists have gotten overconfident, and it's up to you and your team to take them down a peg or two. During an economic summit in Switzerland, a group of unknown terrorists take the members of the Venezuelan delegation hostage. Unless the Venezuelan government meets the terrorists' demand—to stop selling oil to the United States—the terrorists will execute their hostages. You need to storm the conference village and eliminate the terrorists. They may have a three-to-one advantage over you, but you still have to clean them up quickly if you want the hostages to live through the night.

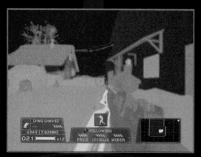

Blanketed in darkness, you want to use night vision or thermal vision to scour the village and spot the terrorists.

Guns & Ammo

Your first mission comes with inexperienced terrorists, but it's still a challenge. The alpine village setting throws some outdoor battles at you early on and then some indoor gunfights. What you need, then, is a primary weapon that can handle both situations.

Look toward the G3A3 assault rifle. With its 3.5x zoom, you can zero in on enemies on the far side of streets easily. Guns like the AK-47 or the SR-2 can't quite give you the necessary visibility in the dark city streets, so you may run into

The G3A3 gives you range and firepower in close quarters.

trouble even with night vision active. The G3A3 also packs a great punch; one bullet can kill a man if you hit near the heart or head. Able to zoom or fire in tight, the G3A3 works well as your main outdoor/indoor weapon while walking the streets or canvassing the buildings.

In reserve, go with the M203 grenade launcher. Your four shots are more than enough to clear some rooms or incinerate an enemy group unlucky enough to be caught milling about. Your last two slots should be filled with two more grenades, such as the flashbang,

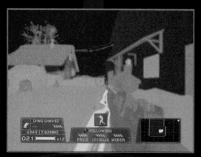

Wipe out enemy groups with the M203 grenade launcher.

to use in the rooms with the hostages or smoke grenades to take advantage of your thermal vision.

Street Smarts

Switch to night or thermal vision before you take your first step. Get used to flipping between regular vision and your special visions to get the best visibility in any given condition. When you've got the hang of it, move to the first building corner.

Take position at the first corner and prepare to battle two enemies at once.

You have two enemies to worry about. The closest threat, to your right and up the hill, should be your priority. If you don't take care of him, he could take care of you when you step out from the corner. You might alert the second guard across the courtyard, but let your teammates deal with him if he shows up.

Thermal vision will probably give you the best target on the first enemy. Peek around the corner and see if he's there. Depending on when you arrive at the corner, he may be exposed at the top of the street or he may be on his patrol down the street and out of sight. If you're confident about your shooting skills, jump out and unload on the terrorist right away. If you want some time to prepare, wait for the terrorist to retreat on his patrol behind the nearby building (he may already be there if he's not in plain sight when you show up at the corner). Zoom in on the street above and clip the terrorist when he walks into sight.

The second enemy will arrive by the wooden fence across the courtyard. There's a path that slants down from the street above to your lower street, and the second terrorist will patrol up and down this side road. Zoom on the top of the path and prepare to fire when the terrorist comes into view.

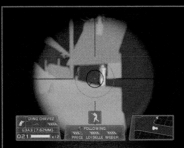

Remove the closest threat first—the enemy patrolling up the hill.

If all the activity with the first guard draws his attention, the terrorist will make a break down the path and hole up behind the car in front of you. Let your teammates lay suppressing fire as you zoom in for a quick headshot that will pick him off cleanly.

The second enemy will patrol the far side of the courtyard and run along the wooden fence to shoot at you from the cover behind the car.

After you've dealt with the first two enemies, you have a choice—take the road to your right, up the hill, or take the slanted path the second enemy came down. You don't want to take the first road. An enemy waits by the 30 kilometer sign and has a perfect ambush point to plunge a couple of bullets into you or your soldiers. Your firepower will overwhelm him, but why absorb unnecessary damage?

You don't want to head up the first street or you'll run into a messy ambush.

Instead, head to the path at the far end of the courtyard. You can walk up to the main road without fear of counterattacks. The one exception: If you shot at the patrolling guard too early and gave him a chance to retreat, he'll be at the top of the slanted path. Look for him just inside the fenced area to your right.

The alpine village streets can seem like a maze the first time you walk them. Stay to your left the whole way and it will eventually bring you to the first terrorist nest and your first objective point. You don't have much to worry about until you pass a red fuel tank on your right (outside the building with the wooden slat walls). Reload at this point—you're about to walk into another ambush.

Stay left through the streets until you hit the first terrorist nest.

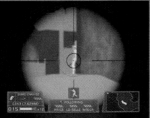

Two enemies lurk in ambush at the corner past the fuel tank.

Zoom at the street corner and go thermal. You'll spot a terrorist with half his body exposed at the corner, waiting for the opportunity to fire into your ranks. Clip him before you enter his field of vision, and watch for his companion to follow up from the right. If you stay zoomed on the area, you should be able to pop him before he figures out exactly where you're hiding. Most of the time, this will end the ambush. However, there is a single guard who patrols the street to the left of the ambush corner. If he hears shooting, he may come to investigate and join in on the festivities.

Kill the terrorist at the end of the street before he returns fire.

Otherwise, the guard to your left will retreat to the far end of the street, just outside the first objective point. This is a much tougher position to battle him in. You have to expose yourself in the street and zoom through debris to set your sights on him. Again, thermal or night vision will give you the best opportunity of spotting the terrorist for a kill shot.

A terrorist tries to get the jump on you from behind the fence to your left.

The terrorists' first nest sits at the end of this street. You don't have to worry about this nest just yet; two enemies hope to take you by surprise first.

To your left, a single terrorist hides behind a fence in a small yard between the two buildings. Don't walk out into the street. You want to stay along the rightmost building, and just as you reach the corner, zoom in on the fence across the street to your left. Hit your thermal vision and pick off your assailant before he can pop out with his automatic weapon.

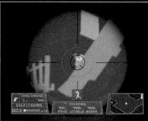

A terrorist sniper looks to whack you from a hidden perch.

The last enemy, before you assault the terrorists' camp, is the hardest to spot. He patrols a roof balcony on the building opposite the terrorists' building. You want to move out across the street and zoom on the rooftop before the sniper finds you. If you're slow, the sniper will kill one or more of your team.

Arrival at the first terrorist camp completes your opening objective.

Close Encounters

Now it's time for some indoor action. Inside the terrorists' building, climb the ladder on the first floor to reach a secluded room on the second floor. Open the door in this room and you'll enter a second empty room. The door in this second room, however, becomes a perfect point to ambush the two terrorists guarding the second floor.

The first-floor ladder gives you a great ambush point for the two second-floor guards.

Open the door and shoot off a burst at the terrorist at the top of the stairs. A second or two after you drop him, a second guard will exit the door to your left. Stay in the cover of the doorway and blast the second terrorist as he jumps out to see what's going on.

A third terrorist waits in the living room downstairs. Head to the top of the stairs and zoom down on the fireplace. You should see the terrorist behind the couch. Zing him before he places you at the top of the stairs. Now the first and second floors are

Eliminate the terrorist in the living room with a sniper shot from the stairs.

clear. You only have the basement to worry about.

You could have your men storm the first floor, then battle the guards on the second floor at the stairwell.

If you don't want to go it alone, you can storm the first floor by skipping the ladder and taking on the guard in the living room first. Send your soldiers in to deal with him, but not in so far that they come in range of the two guards upstairs. When the living room guard has been dispatched, inch along the stairs and zoom up to get a peek at the second-floor guard. Snipe one, then move out in front of the stairs to pick off the second.

This approach will be more challenging than ambushing the second-floor guards. It's only recommended if you've already taken wounds and don't want to try the ambush on the second floor up close and personal.

Douse the cellar with a phosphorous grenade to clear the way.

There are two terrorists in the cellar. Switch to your secondary weapon, the M203, and launch a grenade down the stairs. If you aim it right, it will explode on the cellar floor and take out the closest guard. Worst case, it will prove a great distraction as you descend the stairs and shoot the terrorists. When you head down the stairs, try to kill the terrorists by firing through the stair slats. If you wait till you hit the basement floor, it will be a difficult firefight and you may take some wounds.

After the grenade, remove any other targets through the stair slats or by heading down below yourself.

Church School

Exit the basement through the two doors that lead out into the back alley. Head right at the first intersection, and you should see a truck parked in front of the alley. Walk to the end of this alley and prepare for sniper crossfire.

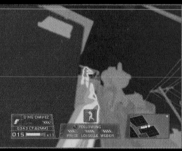

Across from the church, a sniper waits on the balcony.

In the church bell tower, a second sniper hopes to catch you in crossfire.

Two snipers guard the street in front of the church. The first terrorist hides in a balcony across the street from the church (up and to your left at the end of the alley). The second terrorist hangs out in the church bell tower. Together, they can mow your team down if you don't lock on to them before they lock on to you.

Two terrorists flank the church's main entrance.

Inch out to the end of the alley and train on the balcony high up and to your left. In thermal mode you should see the terrorist before he signs his flashlight down on you. Snipe him before you step out too far and expose yourself to the bell tower assassin.

After the balcony sniper falls, slide out to the left and pick off the bell tower sniper. Make sure the truck stays between you and the street, since you have two more terrorists on the other side.

The first street guard patrols by the church's side entrance, left of the truck. He will either be at the building corner or hiding behind the lumber pile in front of the side entrance. The second street guard walks the street to

Assault the church from the side entrance.

the right of the main entrance. Zing the side entrance guard first, then step out into the street and gun down the second terrorist.

While you prepare outside the church's doors, study the map for some valuable information about the interior layout.

Use the church's side entrance as your assault point. You don't want to announce yourself through the front door, do you?

There are four enemies guarding the first hostage in the church itself, so you need to perform a Zulu maneuver so you

can lay siege to the church from two different positions. Set your men to "breach and clear on Zulu" for the door opposite the church's side entrance door. You take the second door. When you're ready, hit the Zulu button and charge in after your team blasts their door off its hinges and starts firing.

Order a Zulu maneuver to lay siege to the church from two different directions.

Your door opens on the walkway running along the church pews. Two enemies guard the door in the corner. Your job is to take these two down before they can

return fire at you or your men. There's a third guard to your right hiding along the pews. Hopefully your squad will gun him down while they breach the front of the church.

The last guard holds a gun to the hostage on the altar dais. Zoom in on him as soon as your two enemies drop, and shoot him before he can put a bullet in the woman you've come to rescue. Secure the hostage and head to the church cellar for the last rescue mission.

The third guard hides in the walkway on the opposite side of the pews.

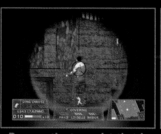

Remove the terrorist that has a gun pointed at the hostage, and you've got one delegate safe and sound.

Open the door to the left of the altar and follow it around to the corridor behind the church.

Watch out for terrorists that jump out at you.

In the second hallway, two terrorists will shoot up the corridor at you. Return fire until they drop. A third terrorist lurks in the door to your right. If any of the terrorists stay in the rooms, shoot off some gunfire and inch down the corridor

until you draw them out into the open. You don't want to hunt them while they have the advantage of the room's cover.

Surprise the two terrorists in the corridor behind the church.

When you count three dead terrorists, head into the big library room on your right and search in the far corner. You should find an old staircase leading to the cellar. The last of the terrorists and the final hostage are down those stairs.

Head down the stairs and turn right when you reach the cellar floor. You must loop around through the rooms to your right and reach the other side before you reach the terrorists' final nest. In the corridor with the bricked-over archway, turn right and you'll be looking straight at the remaining four terrorists.

Try to lure the terrorists out from the rooms for an easy kill in the hallway.

When you assault the final basement room, do not use grenades. The hostage will get injured and the operation goes down the tubes.

Go thermal and wait for the first terrorist to charge. He'll make a break for the barricade in the corridor and try to shell you. When he comes up to shoot, he'll expose his head and upper torso. Clip him quickly and move past the barricade for a clean shot at the rest of the room.

The first guard will step to the barricade and attack.

To your right, a second terrorist holds a gun on the last hostage. Two other terrorists comb the back of the cellar room, making the best of the available cover. Look for their heat signatures to pop out from behind the room's furnishings. Gun down the two "hidden" terrorists from the relative safety of the corridor. If you don't spot them right away, you may have to charge the room to prevent them from plugging the hostage.

During the attack, switch to thermal if you have trouble locating the enemy.

The fourth and final terrorist will pay more attention to the hostage than to you unless you charge into the room. Slip out from the wall and trigger a burst that separates the terrorist from his boots. Be careful not to spray the hostage by accident.

Finish off the last terrorist to rescue the second hostage and call it a night.

Once you secure the second hostage, the mission is a success. Take a breather, but don't rest too long. Some of the terrorists managed to escape the Swiss police. Your second mission will be to do what you do best—stop the terrorists before they do further harm.

MISSION 2: MOUNTAIN HIGHWAY

They got away. At least some of the terrorists you battled in the alpine village managed to slip through the cracks. During their escape attempt, they wiped out in a commuter tunnel. The Swiss police have them surrounded, but the terrorists have rigged a bomb to explode if the police decide to charge in. For good measure, the terrorists have taken two hostages to hold as bargaining chips. Deactivate the bomb, rescue the hostages and you can finally ask for a good night's sleep.

The chopper drops you one hill away from the bad guys.

Guns & Ammo

The terrorists are sitting on a bomb. You don't want them setting that off, and they will if they sense you coming. With the .45 caliber UMP, you can avoid this problem. Its 2x scope works decently in the outdoors, which you only have to worry about in the very beginning, at the tunnel mouth. The rest is medium to close range, and the UMP fires very well within those parameters. However, its biggest gift to you will be its suppressed fire. A submachine gun that shoots silenced bullets can inflict heavy casualties, and the enemy won't even know it. When you storm the tunnel for the bomb, you shouldn't raise much of an alarm if you take point and eliminate all tunnel hostiles quietly.

For backup, take along a M203 HE or M203 RP. There will be instances where you may need to clear a room of terrorists. Just be careful the hostages aren't anywhere nearby. In the three and four equipment slots, try a flashbang grenade and tear gas grenade. Now you have two more weapons to flush out entrenched terrorists.

You don't want to charge into the main tunnel with a loud submachine gun and alert the whole place.

Tunnel Vision

The hardest terrorist to spot guards the tunnel mouth from the top left office window.

From the insertion zone, hug the hill to your left and walk out until you can spot the police lights. You don't want to approach too close or the terrorists guarding

the tunnel will spot you. You do want to inch out far enough to get a clear shot at the corner of the tunnel's office section.

If you zoom on the top left window, you'll spot the terrorist who could conceivably give you the hardest time. He's in perfect position to gun down anyone who attempts to cross the open pavement in front of the tunnel. You must pick him off before going any farther.

Use the cars in front of the tunnel as a screen to reach the terrorists on the other side.

Several terrorists patrol the area in front of the tunnel. You'll have to pay close attention so you don't get caught in any unexpected crossfire. Usually, two enemies sit on the other side of the brown SUV parked perpendicular to the tunnel mouth. Slide along the perimeter and keep the SUV between you and the lighted tunnel mouth. This should provide enough cover to jump up and surprise the terrorists.

When the shooting has diminished, flick to night vision and peer into the garage below the first office window. One or two terrorists like to spring out of there, and if you don't have night vision on, they will get off a few shots before you locate their exact position. Without the darkness, they don't stand a chance, so gun them down as soon as they step out.

Switch to night vision if you can't see through the thick shadows.

Call up your team to deactivate the bomb in front of the downed tractor trailer. You have to be careful, though; the enemy has an ambush planned. As soon as your team reaches the "safety" of the tunnel mouth, rush up in front of the bomb so you have a clear shot at the area under construction by the steps.

The bomb lies in front of the downed tractor trailer.

An enemy will try to machine gun you down from behind the drape over the construction materials.

One enemy will strike at you from behind the drape over the construction site. As soon as you see movement, unload on the curtain and keep up the barrage until there's no chance of return fire, or worse, a grenade in your lap.

The second wave of the ambush erupts out of the tunnel's side doors.

The second part of the ambush will hit your team from the side doors. If your men are positioned correctly, they should mow these two terrorists down before they have a chance to shoot or pull a grenade pin. After a few seconds, if there is no more movement, the ambush is over. You've shut down the bomb and completed the first part of the mission.

Office Firings

Leave your team for a second and head up to the side door the terrorists attempted the ambush from. No sense risking your team for this encounter.

Watch out for the lingering enemy in the side corridor. He likes to roll a grenade as a welcoming mat.

Position yourself so you can slide into the corridor beyond with a flick of the joystick. Depending on how many enemies joined in on the ambush, there may be another hiding in this corridor—and he's dangerous. His first inclination is to chuck a grenade at you. If you don't get the jump on him, you may need to duck back out the door and around the corner to avoid eating shrapnel. Once you have him sighted, drop the terrorist and call up the rest of your team.

Take out the two terrorists in the parking garage.

The next door leads to the parking garage. There are two terrorists on the far side, and you'll have to switch to either night or thermal vision to catch a glimpse through the posts and piping. From the doorway, snipe the first terrorist. Slide to your left down the stairs, keeping your gun trained on the area behind the first dead terrorist. The second enemy should appear as you cross toward his platform. Drop him like his friend before him.

 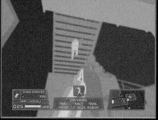

When you see the terrorist's shadow on the stairwell wall, switch to thermal to better identify his position.

Head through the door in the parking garage and then to a second door in the corridor beyond. When you open this door, notice the shadow of a terrorist on the wall. It's a clue that he's waiting for you up the stairs. If you charge blindly up those stairs, he'll gun you down like a dog. Switch to thermal so you can see his heat signature through the stair slats. Back into the far lower corner and train your sights on the middle stairwell platform. When the guard comes down for a look, blast him like there's no tomorrow.

On the second level, prepare for some interference in the office area. One guard patrols at the far end of the office corridor. Open the door and fire a quick spurt down the corridor. If your aim is true, it will either down the guard or incapacitate him enough for you to zero in with another burst.

Nab the lone guard at the end of the office corridor.

Use the first office to surprise the terrorist by the security monitors.

Take the door to your right. It holds an office window overlooking the outdoor tunnel mouth. In fact, it's where you picked off the very first guard, so you know that the adjacent room holds another office. If you were perceptive, you may have noticed TV monitors flickering in that room, signaling a security station of sorts. And what respectable terrorist organization seizes a complex and doesn't plant a guard at the security station?

The answer: none. Throw open the door and—surprise—one of the terrorists waits in front of the security panels. From your side angle, you can aerate him before he has a chance to turn.

Leave by the door in the security office and head to the door on the opposite corridor wall. There's one last terrorist hidden in this room, and he's not exactly friendly. When you open the door, you had better be quick. It's like an old-fashioned high noon showdown, and the one with the fastest draw goes home the winner.

Clean up the last guard in the office area.

Your toughest fight comes in the large construction area. It holds four enemies you must account for.

Your toughest fight is up next. In the large room under construction, four enemies have great position. One stands on the construction scaffolding with a clear shot at your door. Two more hide beneath him amidst the wood boards and plastic sheets. A fourth will hit you from the open doorway at the end of your walkway after the firing starts.

You want backup on this firefight. Click to send your three men onto the walkway, about halfway down with the wood boards as cover. As soon as you do, duck around the corner yourself and unload on the guy atop the scaffolding. He has the best shot at you initially, so you want to eliminate that threat.

Watch the far walkway doorway. If an enemy pops up and your team doesn't spot him right away, you're going to have to shoot past them and hit the terrorist. One mistake and you'll amputate one of your comrades instead, or miss the approaching terrorist and he might do it for you.

The last two terrorists will come out after the firing starts, but you have a few seconds before they act. Go to thermal and you'll be able to trace their bodies through the obstacles. Help your teammates remove them from play.

A sniper watches the upper level of the large garage, while more terrorists patrol the bottom level with the hostage.

In the next room, ignore the door to your left for a moment. Plant your team in the room, just in case an enemy decides to pop up from downstairs, but you really want the door to your right, which opens on the larger parking garage.

Punish any enemies you see so they don't raise the alarm.

You come in on a walkway above the large parking garage. Your first worry comes from the walkway on the opposite side. As soon as you enter, a terrorist sniper runs for a better shooting position. If you don't hit this terrorist on the move, he'll shoot you dead in two shots.

Below, two or three terrorists guard the hostage (out of sight to your left). You want to eliminate these guards from your higher vantage point. It's much easier than trying to fight them all on the ground. Watch out for a second terrorist on the high walkway. He has a tough time shooting at you through the concrete columns, but you will have to deal with him in the end.

If they haven't been alerted, you can find one terrorist on his cell by the lumber stacks. The last terrorist waits in the back of the idling truck by the hostage.

Head back into the previous room, through the unopened door, and down the stairwell. It takes you to the room adjacent to the parking garage. If you haven't made too much noise, you'll find a terrorist here talking on his cell phone. Drop him, but watch out for others. The terrorists move around well, so you can find

different numbers in this room and the parking garage. You may find a terrorist immediately to your right as you enter the room, behind a stack of wood.

Enter the parking garage and zoom on the truck with its headlights on at the far end. A terrorist will pop up here to try and machine gun the lot of you. Snipe him before he can trigger off any rounds. Double-check that your earlier sweep from above has cleared out the place, and walk over to the alcove on the left. You'll find your first hostage tied up against the wall.

Once your team gives the all clear sign, you've rescued your first hostage.

The Back Door

Now you want the second hostage out in the tunnel. The terrorists have barricaded the back half of the tunnel so the police can't get to them. Little do they know that you're using the back door.

A sneaky terrorist attacks from above.

Before you get there, though, you need to fight four more terrorists. The first two will put some lead in your back if you're not extremely careful. In the area with the idling truck, watch for a terrorist high up and to your left. He'll wait for you to move in the corridor and then try to pick you off. When you leave from the hostage, bring your whole team, and that amount of bullets should stop him. In the next corridor, a sniper sits up in the rafters waiting for you to pass below. Watch for the gap in the ceiling and walk with your gun pointed back over your shoulder. You only have a split second to turn him into paste before he returns the favor.

Assault the two terrorists in the last room before the back door to the tunnel.

Keep going until you reach the storage room with a bunch of stacked crates and some construction scaffolding. Two terrorists camp here, one behind the crates near the door and a second as backup in the rear of the room. From the doorway, try to nip the first guard before he retreats into a defensive position. The second guard will charge up and look for some cover. Act quickly and you may catch him by surprise in the open walkway.

A silenced weapon comes in handy while picking off the remaining terrorists in the tunnel.

Weave through the last few doors until you open on fresh air. There will be a guard directly in front of you. Your silenced UMP really comes in handy here, since you can down terrorist after terrorist without alerting the ones farther ahead. Drop the first guard, then step out into the tunnel and pick off the guard directly around the truck barricade.

Weave through the tunnel cars and eliminate resistance.

Bounce from car to car and pick off the remaining terrorists in this section. You should surprise most of them, and the ones that you don't, you'll know exactly where they are since it's such a confined space. Until you reach the sideways truck, you should motor smoothly.

Your last terrorists stake out the position behind the truck.

When you have an angle on the space that leads past the sideways truck and into the last section of tunnel, hold tight for a minute or two. You may catch a terrorist making a dash for the truck's cover, and you don't want to get nipped by any hidden terrorists. When you're sure the area on this side is clear, launch an all-out attack on the two or three terrorists guarding the final hostage.

The terrorists can't withstand your onslaught. Be careful not to hit your hostage by accident, and you'll be calling in the police soon enough. Finally, you can dust your hands of the alpine village terrorists, or can you? Is there a bigger terror threat at work?

Call in the police. You've saved the second hostage.

Just when it seems the terrorists had gone away, they're back. Demanding an end to Venezuelan oil shipments to the United States, they've seized an oil refinery in Curacao and threatened to blow up the complex and kill the facility's manager if things don't go their way soon. Not only *aren't* things going to go their way, but they're going to go very wrong for the terrorists soon enough.

An oil refinery can make for some explosive situations.

Guns & Ammo

Based on accuracy and power, the M16A2 makes the most sense in the dangerous refinery conditions.

Should you misfire inside the refinery, you're in for a world of hurt. There are barrels throughout the facility full of explosive oil; spark one of those with a stray bullet and the explosion will kill anyone in the immediate area. Knowing that, go in with the M16A2. It's the most accurate of the assault rifles, deals solid damage and has a 3.5x zoom for your outdoor skirmishes or for searching through a large room for hidden enemies.

No grenade launchers in here. Instead, bring along the dependable Desert Eagle pistol, just in case you run out of ammo inside the refinery. The flashbang and tear gas grenades are non-lethal alternatives in areas where you might find hostages.

Bombs Away

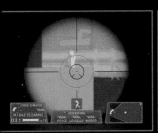 

Search out the outdoor guards with your thermal vision. Find the nearby oil barrel and spark up a conflagration.

Two guards patrol the rooftop you start on. They're around the corner to your left, behind a series of barrels. Flick on thermal vision and you should see them better than the normal night gloom.

You can shoot it out with them, but there's an easier way. Look for the barrel behind the closest guard. This barrel holds explosive oil that will go up like a volcano when you hit it with a stray bullet. Rather than leave it to luck, aim for the barrel straight away. The explosion will kill the two terrorists and warm you up a bit, but with no lasting damage.

Two terrorists will try and stop you in the generator room.

Take the first door on your right. You'll enter an empty room, which you can use to gather your group and make sure you're all ready to go. Move to the far door in that room and kick it open, with night vision on to see better.

Tip

If an enemy has partial concealment behind cover, switch to thermal to better see the exposed area.

Shoot the enemy directly in front of you. A second terrorist will come from your right. You'll have to knock him down with a shot over the barrels he's using as cover, or wait for him to round the corner where you dropped his companion. Ignore the stairwell to your left and use the door around the corner and to your right.

Use your Zulu command to breach the door to the security office and attack on two fronts.

Past the door, you'll see a stairwell with two doors on the second level. Set a Zulu breach command on the right door, while you prepare to charge in the left door. The breach should disorient the terrorists on the other side long enough to get a much-needed jump on the first round of gunfire. The terrorist in the right corner might cause problems if he can use the cover to shield himself, and the terrorist through the open doorway to your right can lay down a lot of grief when you don't know he's there.

Watch for terrorists hidden in the rear of the office or out in the side corridor.

Your first bomb sits "unguarded" out in the corridor to your right. You don't want to send your demolitions expert over to deactivate it. There are two terrorists waiting on the other side of the fence behind the bomb. If you head over to shut down the bomb now, you'll be peppered with lead. Better to swing around the corner and surprise the enemy with an attack on their hiding place.

At the door behind the bomb, pull it open quickly and gun down the first terrorist standing there. A second terrorist proves a very difficult target as he squats to the left inside the doorway. He will get a shot off at you unless

You've found the first bomb, but you aren't going to deactivate it just yet.

you're very, very fast. You may want to roll a grenade into the room to soften up the defenses so you don't take any damage.

Pick off the terrorists waiting for someone to come along, and try and deactivate the bomb.

Now you can head back and deactivate the bomb. While your demo expert shuts it down, watch the door you haven't tried yet. Right after the bomb winds down, a terrorist will kick open this door and charge in. Train your sight on the door and you won't have a problem.

Kill the terrorist who charges out of the door near the bomb.

Short Fuse

Thermal and night vision will ferret out the enemies in the room with the chain-link fencing.

The room after the first bomb holds only the one terrorist, who should have already charged in at you. Cross to the nearby stairwell, then down to the next closed door. Switch to thermal before you enter the next room, since you have lots of shadow and lots of obstacles.

Two more terrorists hide in the room adjacent to the second bomb room.

A chain-link fence runs in front of you. Take one step into the room and sidestep to your right, training your gun on the heat signature through the fencing. Near the right side of the room, the fence ends and you'll be able to shoot the terrorist. Another stands behind him, and a third will fire from the doorway halfway into the room on your left. Concentrate on the terrorist behind the downed first terrorist, and let your team—which should be following directly behind you—open up on the third terrorist.

Tip

It's possible to shoot through chain-link fence, but not recommended. The majority of the time the shot will be deflected to no effect.

Two more terrorists hide in the next room. Step to the open doorway and zoom on the far side. Pick off the first guard by the barrels and slide into the room with your sights waiting for the second terrorist to expose any part of his body.

Your team flashbangs the one door to the bomb while you fire through the second door.

Two doors (one in the chain-link fence room and the second in the room with the two hidden terrorists) lead into the second bomb room. On the right door, set your team to flashbang on Zulu. The flash grenade should blind the terrorists long enough to eliminate the troublesome ones. You take the left door and prepare to launch open the door *after* the flashbang grenade goes off.

You have several problems in the second bomb room. First, the terrorist in the left corner (standing on the stairs) will immediately jump down to the bomb in front of him and set it off. If you give him more than a few seconds, he'll set off a suicide explosion that will kill everyone else too. Shoot him first no matter what.

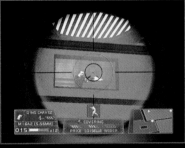

Kill the two terrorists in the upper windows before they kill you.

Second, two more terrorists defend the bomb on the ground floor. Your team should handle these two without much effort.

Third, a terrorist sniper stands at the two windows high up in the room. The central window allows him to shoot down on either door, so as soon as you kill the suicide bomber, aim for the sniper in the window. Left for too long, he will unload a clip and kill at least one of your team. The second sniper has a tougher angle to hit your team (he has a better angle at you in the left door). Turn your attention to him last when all else is quiet.

When the five terrorists are dead, clip the second bomb so no one has to worry about the facility going up in a fire cloud. Your second objective is complete. All you need now is to save the facility manager's skin.

Eliminate the second bomb once the shooting stops.

Oil's Well That Ends Well

Even though the gunfire has died down in the aftermath of the second bomb firefight, there still may be a single terrorist waiting for you in the corridor leading out of the room. He waits in the corner and will fire should you casually wander in that direction. Assume he hasn't been lured into the previous fight and let fly a single burst as you round the corner.

Splatter the terrorist at the corner near the second bomb.

RAINBOW SIX 3

Wind through the corridor and up the outdoor stairwell on the far side. Go into caution mode when you see the door on the second level. If you walk straight over to it, you won't walk through it. There's an assassin waiting up on the roof behind you. Stay flat against the wall by the stairs, then train your sight on the area between the two smokestacks, just above the roof ledge. Eventually, your assailant will come into view.

A sniper looks to surprise you from the rooftops.

Scare the terrorist away from his crate cover and mow him down in the open corridor.

When you open the door, the two terrorists inside will react immediately. One will try to gain the cover of the crates around the corner to the right. The second will use the wall as cover. The terrorists will expose their backs in that second as you enter, so spray some lead in their direction. You want to try and push the first terrorist away from the crates and toward the open corridor. If he gets entrenched in the crates, it's a much more difficult shot to take him down.

Flank the computer room and wipe out the terrorists inside before they can run for help.

Pass through the far door and into a U-shaped room. There's a door on the right, and another on the left that leads outside to a second door. Both the right door and the second left door lead into a computer room

Set your team to frag the room on Zulu. You need to get into position on the left door. Wait for the grenade to detonate, then push open the door and gun down the terrorist behind the control panel. Your team should take care of the other two. If not, blindside whoever returns fire.

Open the door in the back of the computer room. Two more guards hang out at the end of the corridor by some crates. Your two-pronged attack should take the computer room team by surprise, so the two support guards won't know you're coming. Two bursts should eliminate them without any friendly casualties.

If you are thorough, the two support guards will not know you hit the computer room.

A big fight breaks out in the tanker courtyard.

Don't open the next door into the tanker courtyard until you're reloaded and ready with a game plan. The enemy is well prepared in the next area. You have a guard set at the top of the stairs, two on the catwalk across the courtyard and two on the ground floor in the corners. Once you enter, they'll all converge on your doorway. Plus, there's another terrorist on the rooftop who will fire from either the left or right side, depending on where he can get the best angle.

Shoot the terrorists up high and down low.

Click on your team to move into the room and pick off the terrorist on your catwalk. Dart onto the catwalk and fire at whatever moves. You may shoot at the two catwalk terrorists, or the two rushing around the ground floor. Concentrate on these four enemies first. The rooftop assassin won't attack until you make some progress on the catwalk, so sit tight and take care of business before you fool around with the lone gunman.

The terrorists defending the hostage are heavily armed.

Caution

If you've taken two or more wounds, let your team do most of the fighting in the final courtyard. Conversely, you may have to do the dirty work if your team is suffering.

If you thought the last fight was tough, wait till you face off against the rocket launcher. The final group of terrorists will try and take you with them should they fall.

Two terrorists assault right away from the barrels in the middle of the courtyard. A third terrorist hides behind barrels to your left when you step into the area. Fire from the doorway; you have a clear path at the first two assailants. When they drop, step into the courtyard and fire to your left to drop the terrorist by the oil barrels.

Three terrorists up high will put on the heat if you step out in the courtyard.

Look above this terrorist and you'll see a machine gun-toting terrorist in the window. Fire back at him and make sure your bullets land more than his. Slide to your left and flick on thermal vision. Across the courtyard, you will see another terrorist on the upper ledge. He will zero in on you quickly, so

don't hold back—you need to drop him like a bad habit. When he falls, a second terrorist will come in from the right and deliver some more firepower from the upper ledge.

Now it gets really tricky. There's still a terrorist around the corner to the right. He carries a full-fledged rocket launcher, and one of those missiles will take out your whole team if it lands in your vicinity. You have to slide out and flank him from a new angle. However, the closer

You'll have to flank the terrorist hidden in the courtyard corner. He's armed with a rocket launcher that can cause tremendous damage.

you get to the far side of the courtyard, the greater the chance of triggering the "secret" room the final four terrorists hold the hostage in. You see, there's a closed bay door in the left corner that will open up when you cross the courtyard's halfway point. What do you do?

When you cross to the courtyard's far side, the leftmost bay door opens and releases a secret wave of terrorists.

Well, you have to be quick on your toes. Move out to the left until you can snipe the rocket launcher enemy in the corner. You can't let one of those rockets fire in your direction. If you have trouble handling the terrorists, you may have to charge in and take your lumps. Run past the middle barrels and shoot everyone in sight, especially the terrorist tucked in the corner with the rocket launcher. Let him shoot and it's sayonara to the whole team.

Hopefully, your team will have your back covered. When the "secret" enemies charge out of their hidey hole, your team should lay into them. Just to be sure, swing back to your left and fire at the two terrorists charging out. After they fall, look for the two remaining terrorists behind the barrels.

At last, the hostage is safe.

There should be no resistance left at this point. Secure the hostage and ready yourself for a chopper pick-up. You might not smile much in this job, but at least half your team gets to take off the next mission.

MISSION 4: ISLAND ESTATE

A luxurious resort home on a beautiful sunny day. Sounds like the perfect vacation getaway, right? It would be if the place weren't infested with terrorists like roaches in rotten woodwork. The terrorist group that caused havoc in your first three missions has decided to up the stakes—they've captured the president of a Venezuelan corporation and his wife and have threatened to execute both if the United States isn't cut off from Venezuela's oil supply. Because a full squad might alert the terrorists, only you and Weber have been elected for this stealth mission. Enter silent and deadly and, unlike the terrorists, take no prisoners.

If only you could enjoy the view.

Guns & Ammo

With only Weber backing you up, you'll want hardware with a lot of tricks to balance out the odds.

Your bosses upstairs say you only get to bring Weber along on this mission. With half a team, you're less likely to get spotted and draw unwanted attention. It also means you have half the firepower you had in the last three missions. Why not choose a different path this time?

Load up a UMP in your primary slot. The submachine gun carries a modest 2x scope, packs 26 damage and a 43 accuracy. Better yet, the UMP (and your backup MK23 pistol) sport suppressed fire, so you can go completely stealth and remove the terrorists one by one without alerting the whole building.

The UMP submachine gun fires suppressed rounds so the enemy will feel them before they hear them.

For those dicey situations inside the house where the terrorists become alert and fortify, you and Weber each wear a gas mask. You can toss a tear gas grenade into the midst of a potential hornets' nest and watch it clear out in a hurry. You'll need all the advantages you can get with only two against the world.

House Guests

Remember, it's only you and Weber, so you won't have the same firepower you normally have behind you. This mission is not about long firefights—it's about in and out, silent and deadly if at all possible. A long firefight

Creep up the side of the house to the back entrance.

may be inevitable at the end—while you wait for the helicopter to arrive—but until then, keep things small and contained or you'll be overwhelmed, or worse, the hostages will be executed.

Head up to the back of the house and use the kitchen door. There's a single guard behind the kitchen counter, so you have to be quick and accurate. Click open the door, step in, and immediately trigger off a headshot. Do that

Open the door and plug the kitchen guard.

and you won't take a shot; otherwise, the guard locks on to your position and gets off at least one shot from behind his decent cover spot. Weber is pretty good at assaulting the space behind doors, so you may want to command him to "open and clear." He probably won't take a hit.

A two-man team moves faster, but may struggle against a room full of enemies.

Inside the house, the light can be a bit suspect. If you're having trouble seeing, switch to night vision. You don't want to give any advantage to the terrorists; they already have a ton more guys than you.

Switch to night vision to battle the three terrorists in the gloomy downstairs hallway.

One terrorist patrols the downstairs hallway. Wait by the corner in the living room and pick him off first. At the sound of gunfire, a second guard will charge out the first door in the hallway (immediately to your right). Don't enter the hallway; catch him by surprise as he leaves the safety of his room. The third guard resides in the room down the hallway (second door on the right). He will exit last, and you should catch him at the end of the hallway before he has a chance to retreat upstairs and warn the other guards. Good work. You've cleared the first section.

Crash the Party

Beware of the grenade the upstairs guard likes to toss down the steps.

When you approach the end of the hallway, a guard from upstairs—who has no doubt heard all the shooting, suppressed fire or not—tosses a grenade down the steps. When you hear Weber call out "grenade" or hear the thump of something heavy as it lands on the carpeting nearby, duck into the last room or retreat back up the hallway. No sense in taking unnecessary damage.

After the grenade scare, edge to the corner by the stairs and peer up to the top left. You should spot the offending guard peeking out from behind the upstairs

wall. You must shoot him before you climb the steps. If you don't, he will cut you into filet mignon.

Two guards will try to catch you in a crossfire when you reach the second floor.

You're about to enter a nasty crossfire. You have a guard to your left—in the first room with the open door—who will trigger off several bursts as soon as you step onto the second floor. The guard to your right waits in a secluded corridor and will fire over and over again with his machine gun. Worse, he can fire under a gap in the stairwell that inflicts damage on you without any chance of retaliation on your part.

The best time to attack an enemy? When he's reloading.

Tie your shoelaces and get ready to motor. You have to be quick on this one. Run up the stairs with your back to the right guard. The same panel that the guard shoots under to sting you on the stairs also protects you just long enough to reach the second-floor living room unharmed. By assaulting in this manner, you point directly at the left guard, who is the more dangerous threat. Exposed in the open living room, you must shoot the left guard before he can lock on you.

When guard number one falls, turn your attention to the second one in the secluded corridor. He's very trigger happy and will send a steady stream of machine gun bullets in your team's direction. Wait until you hear him run out of ammo. While he's reloading, step into the corridor and plug him good.

Tear gas takes care of the first set of guards holding the president's wife.

Past the dead guard, there's a door that leads into a new hallway. At the end of this hallway, a single terrorist waits for any sign of disturbance. When you step into the hallway, he does a somersault to his left and escapes to warn the other terrorists holding the president's wife hostage.

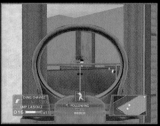

Finish off anyone still lingering in the tear gas.

You won't sneak into this fight. Instead, switch to one of the tear gas grenades you've brought along for just this sort of occasion. Chuck a single grenade down the hallway that the first guard disappeared into. If the terrorists are sharp and keep winging you when you step out into the hallway, you may want to try the bedroom door that opens about halfway down this hallway. From that angle, you can usually plunk a tear gas grenade down at the end of the hallway with a short throw.

Let the tear gas billow for a few seconds; this should drive the guards into hacking fits or make them flee their position. Step back into the corridor with your fully loaded UMP. Depending on how much turmoil has taken place, there should be three or four terrorists here: one in the small alcove to the left, two around the corner to the right. The guard that somersaulted for help may or may not be there; if you're fast enough you can shoot him when you first step into that beginning hallway.

Quickly eliminate the two terrorists holding the wife at gunpoint.

After the tear gas dissipates, head down the corridor and climb the stairs to the right. A door opens into an empty bedroom; however, the door in that bedroom opens into a rather large bathroom that holds the wife and her two guards. Since you don't want her executed, bash in the door and shoot

them one, two. If you're having trouble, command Weber to perform an "open, flash and clear" maneuver, which will leave the wife temporarily blinded, but the terrorists permanently dead.

Presidential Sweet

After you rescue the wife, you have an additional worry: You must not let an assailant shoot your innocent charge.

Secure the wife and be careful—she tags along, so you have to watch that combat fire doesn't clip her. If she dies, the mission fails and you must start again.

Guards may retreat to more defensive positions if they're alerted. You'll have to look for the best angle to ferret them out.

You may encounter a few guards still milling about this area, especially if they were forced to flee from the tear gas. Be on your toes to clip anyone who appears.

When you leave the bedroom, head down the stairs to your right. Usually, there is a single guard at the bottom of the stairs. He likes to use the wall as cover and barrage the stairs as you descend. Let him. A good trick is to let him waste his bullets on the stairwell—you rarely take even a single hit—and when he's out of ammo, turn the corner and let him have it back. Shoot fast enough and he won't have a chance to reload and counterattack.

The room before the courtyard holds a single guard.

Pass through the large room with the piano and look to your first door on the left. A single guard waits to kill the next person he sees. Jump into the doorway and shoot before he does. You can assault the upcoming outdoor courtyard from either the door in the guard's room or the door in the room to your right. The left door (by the dead guard's body) provides more cover, so you may want to slip through there.

Two more guards charge at you in the courtyard.

Open the door and survey the courtyard quickly. You have a door to your immediate left, one almost diagonally across the courtyard from you, and a balcony high up and to your left. All three of these places contain enemies you must deal with.

The first enemy charges at you from the far door. You must be aware of him, though he takes a while to reach you, so turn your attention to the immediate left door. Try to blast the terrorist that steps out of that door before he reaches the cover of the nearby pillars. After you burst a few in his direction, swing back to the guard charging across the courtyard. If you're smooth, you can drop both without a single enemy shot returning fire.

Look to pick off the balcony assassin from either of the two doorways that open on the courtyard.

The balcony guard is much tougher to take down. Walk, even run, across the courtyard and you're dead meat. You must kill the assassin before you can travel farther.

The courtyard's left door provides great protection from the balcony assassin. Of course, this means you have a tricky shot to clip him up there. The right door opens with a great angle on the balcony; however, open the door at the wrong time and the assassin will kill you before you have a chance to aim. The less risky play is to attack from the left; you just have to wait patiently for a glimpse of the assassin through the stone obstacles.

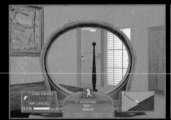

Zing the outer guard before opening the door into the last hallway and killing the next two terrorists.

Cross to the other side of the courtyard and open the door there. You enter an empty room that holds an open door into another room. Through that open door, you should spot a single terrorist guarding the area. Clip him from this range, since you don't want to get into a close-combat shootout with a man in better cover than you.

Open the door behind him and clean up the two terrorists in the hallway. One holds the corner, while the other may take cover behind the plant down the hall by the courtyard door. These are your last two threats *inside* the house.

Too slow and the president dies.

The door at the end of the hallway opens into the final courtyard. One enemy to your left watches over the president. You must engage him immediately. Ideally, you want to take him down with one short burst, but, at the very least, you need to draw his attention to you. If you don't, he will execute the president without hesitation.

Pop the guard in the final courtyard to save the president—for the time being.

Hold On for Dear Life

Prepare for an onslaught of terrorists who will get in your face and shoot you.

You've freed both hostages. You're home free, right? Wrong. The helicopter can't get in until you clear up the last attackers, and there are a lot coming at you in this courtyard.

Tip

You can't afford to protect the hostages by putting your bodies between them and the terrorists. Leave the hostages be and concentrate on killing any assailants from the protection of the doorway.

Don't forget about the balconies. Some of your most dangerous threats come from above.

Contrary to what you might think, you can't protect the hostages here. Yes, you will ultimately protect them by killing all the remaining terrorists, but if you worry about the hostages' safety in the middle of this giant firefight, you will not survive. What you want to do is back into the doorway so the walls shield you, and you can only be hit from someone already in your arc of fire—meaning, you will have a chance to plug them before they plug you. If you have time, try to "push" the wife between you and Weber so she stays shielded a bit.

Zoom in and out to get the best fix on potential enemies.

Make sure Weber is right by your side, and together you should unload on anything that moves. Try to be as

accurate as possible. You may find yourself low on ammo with more than a dozen enemies to kill here, especially if you went hog wild earlier. If you have to, switch to your MK23 pistol; it has a shorter range, but at least it shoots bullets.

You may have to switch to thermal to lock on to enemy targets.

Two enemies will attack you down low and try to get in close, one to either side. Blow them away, and then look to the balcony high up and to your right. Two enemies will attack from there, and one terrorist will try and drop a grenade down on your head. If that falls, you can kiss the hostages, and probably yourself, good-bye. Let Weber lay down cover fire across the courtyard while you make sure those balcony guards don't get creative.

You may want to go to thermal to pick up heat signatures. Even though it's daylight, it can sometimes be tough to spot who's firing at you with all the cover spots to scan over. The heat signatures stand out easily.

Eliminate the terrorists on the lower level first. They will have the best chance of seriously wounding someone in your party, unless you think an obstacle provides enough cover that you can slip up top and pick someone off on the balcony. Throughout the battle,

At last, the helicopter arrives to chauffeur you to safety.

you should concentrate on the right side while Weber concentrates on the left. From the protection of the doorway, you have a great angle on the right side of the courtyard, but not so good on the left. At some point, you will have to step out to help Weber clear the left side (especially those terrorists nestled around the corner to your left). Don't try this maneuver until you're sure the right side has been completely cleared.

Tip

If you have any tear gas left, throw it all around the courtyard to hamper the buzzing enemies.

Eventually, you will hear the chopper blades and dust will kick up. That signifies you're close. You probably only have three or four more enemies to go. Usually these stubborn souls are hiding up on the balcony, to your left around the corner. Wipe those last enemies out and you can deliver the president and his wife to another, safer, vacation home.

MISSION 5: SHIPYARD

You face a triple bomb threat, and if you aren't careful you're going up with the rest of the shipyard. The same mysterious terrorist group that has plagued an alpine village and island estate has staked out a Venezuelan shipyard. As a reliable terrorist organization, they have wired the whole facility with explosives, ready to detonate at the first sign of trouble. You're all about trouble, just not the kind they'll see coming.

You begin outside on the main docks.

Guns & Ammo

[Fo]r variety and versatility, we'll take along the L85A1 [a]ssault rifle on this mission. It's manufactured with fine [ra]nge and damage scores, and has one of the better [ac]curacies for assault rifles. Since you'll need to make [s]ome long-range shots on the mission, we opted for the [L8]5A1's 3.5x scope. Another plus: It runs 30-round [cl]ips, so you shouldn't come up short on ammo.

The L85A1 gives you range, damage, and accuracy.

As backup, take the M203 HE or M203 RP. There will [b]e certain combat hot spots, such as the first battle on [t]he docks, where a little extra bang could shake things up [i]n your favor. For interior battles, the flashbang and tear [g]as grenades can stir the enemy into vulnerable positions.

Shadows and Snipers

[Y]our first arena will be the docks and their 30-foot-high [c]rate piles. It makes for a maze that hides you well and [h]ides your enemies just as well. Be careful while [n]avigating the twists and turns—enemies will get off a [f]ew more shots than normal in these confines.

Don't let the initial terrorist escape or you're going to have

Turn right from your insertion zone and right again at the stack of crates. This will bring you to a hot corner, where three enemies await. The first one patrols this side of the docks, as well as the far side, so you may not see him right away. The second and third terrorists play assassin on the top of the crates.

Wait for the first terrorist to stroll out into view from the opening between the crates. As soon as you gun him down, a second terrorist will appear on the crates to the right. Aim about 10 feet off the ground and you should strike true. The third terrorist sometimes fires from the stairs behind the crates, way up high. You may avoid him altogether if you move in closer; his field of vision won't spot you if you're standing near where the first terrorist dies.

The gap between the crates on the left side leads to the second half of the dockyard. A big pile of crates lies in the center of this area, and the terrorists have entrenched themselves around the cover. From the gap, you will spot the first one to the left of the crates. Zoom in and take care of him.

Look for a second sniper high up on the dock crates.

Zoom and snipe the guards to the left and right of the central crates.

Slide along the crates and wait until the first terrorist on the right side shows a shoulder or leg. Shoot a burst or two to take this one down. Don't go any farther until you knock this guy out of contention.

A single terrorist hides up on the crates to your right in the second dock zone. Walk out without preparation and he'll rattle a few slugs through you.

The second terrorist on this side is much tougher to deal with. He stands atop a crate and has a perfect angle on the entry point to this area. If you blindly walk out into the open, he will paint the ground with your innards. Turn to face the crates on your right side and sidestep out into the open when you're ready. As with the previous sniper, you want to fire about eight to 10 feet up in the air. With a little luck, you may down the tango before he tags you.

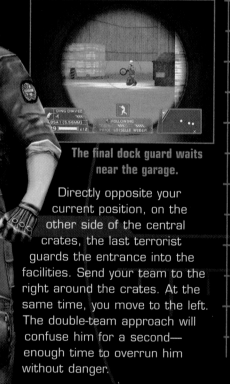

The final dock guard waits near the garage.

Directly opposite your current position, on the other side of the central crates, the last terrorist guards the entrance into the facilities. Send your team to the right around the crates. At the same time, you move to the left. The double-team approach will confuse him for a second—enough time to overrun him without danger.

Terrorists look to get the drop on you in the office or the stairwell to the second floor.

Move straight through the garage and open the door in the back. You've entered a small office with long, horizontal windowpanes. Don't walk too far into the room. If you or your team crosses in front of the windows, an enemy sniper will fire and probably kill the unfortunate with a headshot. Instead, take the doorway to your right and head down the corridor.

Reload in here; you've just fought through a big battle and may be low on ammo. Get ready and open the door. There's a terrorist aiming at the door on the other side. The split-second surprise might be enough to drive him back with a quick barrage. If you don't hit him right away, duck to the right and use the doorjamb as cover. When he pauses, duck back and fire with a better idea of where he's standing.

Enter the upstairs office and drop the first terrorist with a perfect shot through open doors.

Climb the stairs and open the door on the second floor. Four terrorists have this office staked out. Set your team to watch at the hallway in front of the door. You head to the left and attack from the second hallway. The idea is for you to scare the enemy so they take up defensive positions on the other side, right into the firing arc of your soldiers.

At the first doorway, peer through the office inside and you should spot a terrorist on the opposite side. Gun him down if your positioned team hasn't already. Another terrorist should be in the same area and will probably fall to your team.

Kill or secure the remaining three terrorists staking out the office.

Two more terrorists wait at the end of the offices, between the two hallways. Round this corner guns blazing; you'll wipe them out, drive them into your set-up team, or force them to surrender.

Send your team to the top level to cover the whole warehouse.

Exit the office and you'll discover your first casualty. The terrorist have gunned down this poor soul and left him here to rot. Step over the body and climb the ladder to the top level. Assign your team to watch over the entire warehouse from this key position on the rooftop.

Superior positioning will eliminate the warehouse terrorists without breaking a sweat.

Drop back down the ladder and head out onto the catwalk that runs around the large warehouse. You should engage some hostiles soon, but don't worry too much with the three guns on the roof. They will eliminate anyone they can see without much effort. The only troops you have to worry about are the ones hidden from your team. Fortunately, the hidden ones are probably hunkered down because they don't want to get shot. You should be able to surprise these few as you assault the lower level.

Whack the last terrorist and defuse the first bomb.

Take things slow on the ground floor and scout around crates and forklifts. There may be one or two terrorists left, and you don't want to get careless and take a slug. After you've snooped the whole area, give the "demo up" command to shut down the first bomb in the middle of the warehouse.

Bomb Sheltering

Intelligence reports that the second bomb lies on the level below the first bomb. Take the stairs in the warehouse area down to the lower level. When you enter the room with the steel mesh wall, turn right and take the door in the corner.

The second bomb lies below the first bomb.

Take out the three terrorists surrounding the second bomb.

You've found the second bomb room already, but it won't be as simple to get to the bomb. Two terrorists hang around the bomb, while a third hides in the corner to your left, behind a stack of crates.

Before they have a chance to react, jump into the room and mow down the two terrorists closest to the bomb. Walk toward the bomb with your sights on the corner with the crates. Pick off the third terrorist as soon as he comes into view.

Quiet the ambush and you can deactivate the second bomb.

Notice that the ceiling in this room holds big bay doors that can swing open. It's part of the ambush waiting for you. When all seems clear and you bring your team around the bomb, the doors will drop from the ceiling and four terrorists (two in each area) will fire down. If you're not prepared, your whole team will be wiped out from this ceiling ambush. You gotta admit, it is kind of clever. Of course, we know it's coming, so as you approach the bomb keep your guns aimed at the bay doors. When they open, you fire, and keep firing until no one moves up there.

Deactivate the second bomb and listen for further instructions. The third bomb lies even farther below the shipyard.

Into the Bowels

Only coordinated positioning will get you through the next ambush.

Exit from the second door in the room, behind the shrink-wrapped crates. Hang a right and keep going until you see a well-lit corridor with two heavy steel doors on either end. You might have had enough of them, but another ambush awaits you, and this one might be worse than the bomb room setup.

If you walk the long corridor, when you reach the center point, both steel doors swing open and terrorists unload in the tight space. Needless to say, you'll be dead. It only triggers once you cross the halfway point, so how do you avoid this death trap?

Simple. Set your team so that at least one of your guys is pointing directly at the first door. You walk down the corridor and zoom on the far door. Your team has your back, so when you hit the halfway point, they shoot the first set of terrorists and you shoot the second set farther down the corridor. Then order them to rejoin you as you descend to the bottom level.

Shoot the first terrorist and use the crates as cover to drop the remaining five.

The room at the bottom of the stairs has six terrorists flanked around the doorway. The first one waits to the left behind some cover and will barrage the door without hesitation. The other five are on the other side of a pile of crates, so you have some time with them.

It's time for another marksmanship test. You have to enter this room and blast the terrorist to your left without the benefit of your scope or an extra second to line up the shot. It's shoot from the hip or don't shoot at all. If you don't kill him with a quick burst, he will kill you.

Once he falls, the other five terrorists can be subdued with a trick. Stand behind the crates to your right as cover. Let them blast away at the crates, but in your crouched stance, they can't hit you. When you hear them reload, stand up and shoot over the low-lying crates and pick them

As you approach the last bomb, you realize you're short on time—a detonator counts down on the final explosives.

off. If you can only get one, crouch down again and repeat when you think the coast is clear.

A lone sniper tries to surprise you by the big sliding doors.

As soon as you step into this room, the countdown clock on the last bomb begins to tick off. You have a minute and 30 seconds to beat all the rest of the terrorists and deactivate the bomb. It's barely enough time.

Don't waste any time. Cross to the other side of the room and watch the bay doors on the far wall for another ambush. This time only a single terrorist shows up. Four against one odds in *your* favor means game over for your opponent.

Attack the far guard, then swing up and shoot the two terrorists who hope to nail you from above.

Find the doorway in the corner of the room and enter the next room. It's empty, so cross quickly and prepare for the room with the last bomb.

If you look past the crates in the last room, you should spot a lone gunman waiting for you to arrive. Take him out and ready your team for a bunch of activity.

One by one the other terrorists fall.

When the first shot is fired, the terrorists mobilize. One or two of them will try and find cover behind the crates in front of you. Leave your team to take care of them. It's dangerous if they get established there, but you have to rely on your team to down some of them.

Your job is to shoot down the two assassins above you. Another set of bay doors—this time above you on the left wall—sets up two terrorists to rain deadly fire down on your unsuspecting heads. It's brain stew if you're not ready for the little surprise. Only after these two terrorists die can you move into the room.

Shutting down the third bomb completes the mission.

At this point, there should be two to three terrorists left guarding the bomb. If you're injured, send your team in to clean up. If you want to protect someone on your team, then you turn the corner and go after the last few around the bomb. If time is running out, click on your team to "demo up," and as they rush to diffuse the bomb, you must intercept the last terrorists.

Finally, you'll cut the last wires on the third bomb and save the installation. The whole Venezuelan government thanks you for saving lives and a couple million gallons worth of oil.

Tom Clancy's RAINBOW SIX 3

MISSION 6: CRESPO FOUNDATION

The terrorists are going after another big player. This time it's Juan Crespo, head of an international children's organization. He's made a lot of antiterrorist statements and has pro-U.S. sentiments, so that puts him on the terrorists' hit list. They tried for Crespo in his Montreal-based headquarters, but missed. However, they did manage to seize the corporate offices and secure several hostages. Your job is to muscle them out of there alive.

Some work needs to be done in the corporate headquarters.

Guns & Ammo

Since we're going door-to-door looking for hostages, now seems like the time to break out the M1 shotgun. Tailor-made for close-combat situations, the M1 will paste any bad guy a body's length away and can spray a roomful of terrorists at once. It doesn't have much range—though the confined quarters nullify that drawback most of the mission—and you have to watch your ammo carefully. The M1 only holds six rounds at a time, and it's a slow reload. In total, you carry just 40 shells for the M1, so don't waste them early in the mission if you can help it.

With a lot of close-quarters combat on its way, the M1 shotgun can smear the carpet with the bad guys.

As backup, bring along the MK23 pistol in case you need to sneak into an area and do some silent killing. Grab a pair of flashbang grenades to shellshock the terrorists, without risking any hostages in the immediate area.

Floor Sweep

From your starting point, head through the doors into the entrance lobby. You get a spectacular view, but no villains yet. Avoid the double doors; you'll get to that hallway soon enough. Take the right door instead; it leads

Catch an enemy from behind and he

into a small office with a single terrorist. He hides around the corner, and as long as the file cabinet doesn't get in your way, you should plaster him with a gut shot.

The guards in the first main hallway use smoke grenades so switch to thermal.

Take the door in this room into the hallway that you would have entered from the lobby's double doors. Two guards stake out the corner of the room across the way. They like to chuck a smoke grenade as soon as they hear you. Let them. You can switch to thermal vision and peer right through the gray cloud, while they can't see. Wait till the smoke thickens then move out and eliminate both of them.

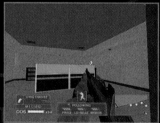

Cut down the two terrorists in the L-shaped office.

Before you reach the end of the hallway, rendezvous outside the door on your right. There are two terrorists in the L-shaped office behind the door. Open it and peg the terrorist behind the cubicles directly in front of the door. Enter the adjoining room and plug the terrorist there before he can dive for some cubicle cover.

In the big office, shoot down the four terrorists, including the one behind the cubicle.

Up the hallway again, take the first door on the right. In this room, four terrorists look to prove a thorn in your side. Two patrol the middle of the floor. One stands behind the cubicles and a fourth squats out of sight behind the far double doors in the room's left corner.

Fire at the two terrorists in the middle of the room. Down them and the one behind the cubicle should duck for cover. While he's hiding, he can't hit you. Slide to the right and watch for the terrorist by the door to come into view. He'll either stay out in the hallway (no threat right now) or more likely swing in around the corner and fire. Bring your whole team in and together your firepower should overwhelm him fast. The last terrorist will eventually pop up to take a potshot at you. Get ready and return fire as soon as you see the head.

Exit the room on the far side by the fourth terrorist and hang a left (the elevator in the hallway doesn't work). Around the next bend, there's a lone gunman in a suit. Shotgun blast him down the hall so you can reach the door he's been guarding.

A well-dressed terrorist guards the final hallway on the first floor.

You charge up the left side in the big computer room and remove the troublesome terrorists behind glass and cubicle walls.

Prepare for a very difficult fight. Inside the big computer room beyond this door, half a dozen terrorists—already behind cover—will open up as you crash the room. You can't really frag or flash the room, since they've bunkered down behind the cubicles on the far side of the room.

You have to lead the charge on this one. Call your team to follow right behind you and click open the door. Run for the left side of the room and aim your shotgun at the single terrorist behind the plate-glass window to your immediate left. That terrorist must go or your whole squad's in desperate peril.

Send your team in to mop up the leftovers.

Keep going after the window terrorist drops. You need to cut around the cubicles and attack the rest of the terrorists from their vulnerable flank. While your team trades fire with them back and forth over the cubicles, the terrorists should stay preoccupied enough that you can line up a shot or three on their exposed sides. Fire a blast, then duck behind the nearby cubicle. Then fire another shot. Switch to thermal so you can see the individual outlines better in the computer room gloom.

Tip

Feel free to use your heavy weaponry, such as grenade launchers, on the first and fourth floors. The hostages are only on the second and third floors.

If you can count five dead bodies (plus the one behind the window), you're probably safe. Send your team deep into the room and let them mop up any token resistance. If the double doors in the back of the room are closed, that could mean that the two guards in the adjacent room haven't joined the fight. Don't take any chances. Command your team to "open and clear" while you stand back ready to plug another maniac if he comes into range.

Carpet Cleaners

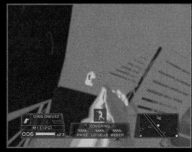

The computer room exits into a cafeteria area. Take the walkway here to the door at the end. When you open this and ascend the stairwell, switch to thermal again. You'll spot a terrorist on a platform that overlooks the second floor.

Trace the terrorist on the stairs through the metal platform with thermal vision.

He will try to maim you as you come up the stairs or wait until you have your back to him while you try the second-floor door.

Train your sights on him and look for an opening between the stairs to pull off a headshot. Don't continue up the stairs until you deal with this threat.

Another terrorist patrols the second-floor walkway.

Be very careful at the second-floor door. If you had trouble with the stairwell guard, then it's probable that the guard on the other side of that door knows you're coming. He'll usually set an explosive charge on the door and blow it to pieces, in the hopes of devastating your team in the process. Keep your team back while you open the door and retreat down the stairs. If there's no explosion, send your team in and hunt him down.

Surprise the terrorists and you may force them to drop to their knees and pray.

A room halfway up the hallway holds two more terrorists. Attack quickly and one or both might surrender to your superior numbers. Remove these terrorists so they don't join the fight when you go for the first hostage.

Flashbang the hostage's room and eliminate the terrorists while they're blinded.

Move up the hallway and take the door to your left. This leads into a small room with another door. Plan your strategy here, since the next door opens into the hostage room.

You have three terrorists guarding the hostage. One holds a gun on the hostage in the back of the room. The hostage kneels in the far left corner; the terrorist

stands in the far right. The two other terrorists mill about in front of the door nearest you.

The best course is to flashbang. You need to stun them so you can eliminate the guard ready to execute the hostage. If you just charge in, you may miss the executioner and lose the hostage. A flashbang usually gives you an extra second or two to bring the three terrorists down.

Search around the hostage thoroughly and remove any threat before setting her free.

After they fall, your work isn't done. There are still terrorists on this level, and you may have one as close as the adjacent room with the vending machine (far right corner). Check to make sure no one will shoot you in the back, then secure the first hostage.

Theater of the Absurd

A lot of glass will shatter while you take on the terrorists in the interconnected offices.

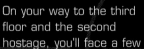

On your way to the third floor and the second hostage, you'll face a few more second-floor guards. Head down the hallway away from the first hostage room and take your first right. This leads into a large room with four offices. You can see into each office through the glass walls, which is a good thing since four terrorists run about this area.

When you enter the area, look left first and shoot if you see a terrorist patrolling the corridor. If not, turn back around and aim into the office in front of you. A terrorist should come into view as he waits in the back corner of that office for a shot at a passerby. Give him the shotgun shells instead.

Let your team set up at the intersection as you wrap around the back. Another terrorist waits in the door to your immediate right. Blow him back with a shotgun blast and continue around to the next opening. The remaining two terrorists like to unload machine gun fire from the back offices. While your team ties them up, look for a clear shot through the windows.

Watch the third-floor hallway for sudden attackers.

When the four terrorists have been dealt with, take the nearby door and pass through the next hallway to the stairs winding up to the third floor. In the third-floor hallway, look right for two terrorists that will try and use the hallway divider as cover.

The second hostage might look like an easy target, but guess again.

The door opposite the stairwell door leads to the second hostage. He's on his knees trapped on a theater stage. Unfortunately, he's got an audience too. A terrorist will pop up in each of the high windows, as well as another one by the far double doors.

You have to be quick to save the second hostage, as terrorists attack from every window and door.

Charge into the room and immediately swing back over your shoulder and aim for the corner window. The first assassin pops up here, and you only have one shot to kill him before he kills the hostage. Get the whole team in on the action so you can cover a lot of ground. Fire up at any of the remaining three terrorists, and don't let the terrorist behind the double doors sneak off

a shot into your back. After an intense minute, you should finally be able to release the hostage.

> ### Tip

You may want to shield the second hostage with your body. He's very vulnerable to the assassins.

Shred of Evidence

Your last task is a short trip up to the fourth floor. Climb the nearby stairs and follow your map until you see the big corner room. Two terrorists watch the cityscape out the window, so you can get the jump on them without much trouble. So much for the front guard.

Two terrorists get a great view in the fourth-floor corner office. Too bad they're not going to enjoy it.

Unload on the terrorists protecting the two that are destroying records.

Press forward and watch your map again. When you get to the room before the final room with the circular objective symbol, reload and ready for a last battle. Charge in and shoot the terrorists in the outer room. Your better numbers and superior marksmanship should doom them.

Reach the back room and kill the evidence-destroying terrorists.

The two terrorists in the back room, who have previously been trying to destroy valuable evidence, will probably come out to see what all the shooting's about. Clue them in and call it a day.

MISSION 7: OLD CITY

One man can blow off the lid on the secret terrorist organization. The informer has information that can help various governments track down the terrorists' illegal activities. One catch: The informer has been taken captive by the terrorists in Dubrovnik, Croatia. Another catch: The terrorists have him at gunpoint and will stop interrogating him and simply execute him if even a peep gets to them that your team has been sent in.

Sun sets on the old city. Let's just hope it doesn't set on our informer too.

Guns & Ammo

For the second time, you've been assigned a two-man mission. Eddie Price accompanies you this time, and the two of you must plow through all the terrorists to reach the informer before harm can befall him. Unlike the last two-man mission, this one is not about stealth. Yes, you have to make sure the terrorists with their guns on the informer don't know you're coming, but the vast majority of the mission will be outside. You have lots of firefights ahead, so you won't have a chance to be quiet. We've opted for damage capabilities and range.

The G3A3 makes a return to our lineup as the best assault rifle in our arsenal.

In the backup slot, carry along the M203 grenade launcher. Again, this is not a true stealth mission. There will be times when the explosive power of the M203 will come in handy. For those times when you may need to distract the terrorists, stock up on flashbang and smoke grenades.

Mean Streets

It's time for another two-man mission. This time Eddie Price accompanies you.

Pull out the G3A3 assault rifle again. As we mentioned before, the G3A3 has an excellent 3.5x zoom, so you can comb the streets and look for assassins around corners and in far windows. The G3A3 also delivers big damage; one burst can kill two enemies at once, if they're close enough together. With the flexibility to fire in tight or at range, the G3A3 is a winner as your main outdoor/indoor weapon.

One, two, three, the terrorists guarding the first plaza go down.

Follow the street from the insertion zone to the first set of steps that leads down into a plaza. You should see a guard with his back to you. An easy target, yes, but as soon as you shoot him, his companion (out of sight to the right) will make a break for it. You don't want him raising the alarm this early, so you need to gun him down before he can do anything annoying. Shoot him as he sprints for the small room straight ahead.

There's still two guards left. Descend the steps slowly and sight on past the corner. Eventually, a guard will come into view, waiting for you to make a move. As soon as you have a sliver of him fixed in your sights, you and Price should make him pay. Another terrorist is in the building to the left at the stairs. Take him out.

Watch for the assassin in the window and the one around the corner in the street below.

Head to your right and down another set of stairs. As you round this bend, notice a block of houses directly in front of you. The second house holds a window, and inside a sniper waits for you to appear. He's got great eyes and will spot you most of the time if you step into view. Should you alert him, he will let loose a barrage and then disappear. He can appear anywhere now, using any of the three windows as a staging point. He has a particularly good shot at you from the window all the way to the right, so do yourself a favor and pick him off before he can really get motivated.

Tip

Thermal vision can detect enemies through stairs and curtains, and you can even spot them on the other side of closed doors.

A second terrorist waits in the street below the sniper's window. He hides at the corner of the building, behind the collection of barrels. Depending on your position and how much combat has occurred, he will either shoot at you from the barrels or dart to the wall on the opposite side and try and clip you when you step out into the street for a better look. Even though you won't go down the street from that angle, wipe him out anyway so you don't have to deal with him again later.

Keep your eyes peeled for two terrorists at the corner and one on top of the building on the left end of the alley.

Continue down the street. No one is in the alley, but there are three terrorists ready at the corner. Slide along the right wall so you can get an angle on the space beyond the corner. You can usually spot the hidden terrorist's leg first, and that should be enough to drop him if you clip it just right. The second terrorist hides out in the small alley off to the right of the main street. A billowing curtain and set of barrels protect him. You can walk past him without a fight if you like, or go in and blast him to continue the clean sweep. The third is up on the top of the building at the end of the alley.

The terrorist in the cellar can chop your legs out from under you. Because of the angle, your best option is a grenade blast.

The sneakiest terrorist is up next. Toward the end of the main street, you'll see a set of stairs heading up to the right where there's a door to a building's second floor. The street continues, but it's that door you want. However, a single terrorist hides out in the cellar window in front of these stairs.

You can't see him until he can gun you down. A piece of roof shields him from view, so there's no gaining a better angle. When you can't pinpoint an accurate shot, it's time to switch to the area-effect attack: the grenade launcher. Volley the grenade into the corner between stairs and broken roof strip and—boom!—instant solution. Even so, face the cellar window as you walk past just in case the lucky terrorist survived and you need to resort to bullets.

Climb the stairs and open the second-story door. You have reached your first objective. Reload and prepare for a few more intense gun battles.

You achieve your first objective when you gain the second house.

Lowdown on the Showdown

In the alley behind the courtyard, two assailants will charge as soon as they catch sight of you.

Find the door on the first-floor in the house with the objective point. Exit into a street and follow it around the bend to your right. You'll see a long straightaway, and two terrorists will begin to charge as you get closer. They'll use barrels and cars as cover. If you zoom and fire as they begin to move, you should catch them out in the open.

Eliminate the remaining terrorists under cover in front of the courtyard entrance.

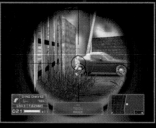

Continue forward. The courtyard you're looking for is off to the right, the entrance is a driveway where the high walls end. First you have to deal with terrorists. Stop just before the broken wooden fence (between the high stone walls on your right) and zoom. You should spot one hiding by the driveway, another to the left between wall and car, and the third will make a break for it and try to use the car as cover.

Shoot the moving target first. Inch in and get an angle on the terrorist by the driveway. After you nick him, slide to your right and do the same to the last terrorist between wall and car.

You're almost ready to assault the courtyard proper. First, though, take advantage of the broken wooden fence. You can actually shoot through it and down one or two of the terrorists waiting for you to enter the driveway. Considering that you'll have to knock off about a dozen anyway, why not cut the odds down now?

Shoot through the slats in the broken wooden fence to pick off a terrorist or two.

As you approach the courtyard, watch out for the sniper dead ahead in the second-story window.

Approach the driveway, but set your sights on the house in front of you at the end of the road. A sniper has your number if you approach too close. Look at the second-floor window, between the palm tree leaves. If you have him in range, that means he has you in range, so snipe him quickly.

Aim high and low and take out all targets before assaulting the courtyard itself.

Position yourself at the front of the driveway, but not too far in. There are three key locations to watch out for, and you'll have to bounce back and forth between them to keep up with the enemy reinforcements.

First, kill anyone up on the roof. They have the best shot at you, so they must be the priority. Through the course of the battle, you may have to remove up to three terrorists from the roof position.

Second, look to the gloomy arches to the left of the van parked in front of the house. It may be tough to spot some of these guys, so switch to night vision if you're having difficulties. You want to remove these threats next, since they have a better angle on you than the terrorists to the right, who have to deal with the big stone wall protecting your right flank.

Third, scan the right side of the driveway, particularly the car parked next to the van. Terrorists like to come up from behind this car to get closer to the action. Cycle through all three of these positions until you feel they're clear. Then, and only then, do you expose yourself on the open driveway.

Wait for the guard to pace in front of the middle window and blast him.

Before you head into the driveway, though, you may want to take out one of the guards inside the house (this just makes it easier for you later when you assault the house). If you wait long enough, you'll see him waltz right past the middle window on the second floor. Time it so you shoot as he steps into view.

Moving into the courtyard, scan right and left for remaining tangos.

Like crossing a major highway, look both ways before committing. More than likely, there will still be a few terrorists off to your far right, since they couldn't shoot at you before with the big wall in the way. Hit zoom and plug them one by one.

Even when you think it's safe, the courtyard is probably not. Check the roof and corners for the last threats.

Continue to look left too. Sometimes a terrorist will make it all the way to far left side and won't come into view until you've walked halfway out in the driveway. Also, don't let a sniper get the drop on you from the rooftop. Check your three prime locations over and over to ensure safety.

Duck inside the first available house door and you've completed the second objective: You've located the informer's building. Now comes the tough part.

When you reach the house holding the informer, you've finished off the second objective.

Lightning Strike

Before you attack the house's inner courtyard, take out the two guards inside.

Inside the house, you have to kill enemies quick and without much fuss. You can't afford for any of the terrorists to surround you and get off multiple shots.

Fortunately, the first two you face are sitting ducks. Follow the corridor down to the right and open the door at the end. You can see a terrorist standing there through a gap in the wall. Pop him and continue to the door on your right. This will wrap you around to the room with the downed terrorist. His companion will come running from the door in the corner. Fire a burst and drive him backward.

Three guards patrol the inner courtyard.

Enter the room the terrorist just charged from and open the far door into the inner courtyard. You'll see two terrorists talking off to your right, and a third either behind some barrels on the far left or out in center. Aim *between* the two terrorists talking and squeeze off a single burst. The G3A3 is so powerful, it kills both terrorists with the single burst. Rotate and gun down the third terrorist before he has a chance to react.

Drop the terrorists on the inner courtyard's balcony level.

Walk out into the courtyard, but don't move into the center. You want to stay under the balconies, since three terrorists patrol these balconies on the upper level and want a shot at you. Switch to thermal if you can't spot them, then walk the perimeter and pick one off at a time. Usually, one stands directly in front of you, another directly above you as you enter, and the third comes running along the rightmost balcony when he hears the firing.

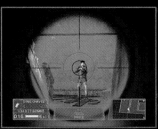

A single terrorist holds the stairs up to the informer's floor.

From the door you entered to the inner courtyard, head to the far right corner and take that door. Go straight and you'll come to the room with the stairs climbing to the upper level. A single guard watches the bottom of the stairs. If you slide in quietly, you shouldn't have a problem.

A single terrorist holds the stairs up to the informer's floor.

From the door you entered to the inner courtyard, head to the far right corner and take that door. Go straight and you'll come to the room with the stairs climbing to the upper level. A single guard watches the bottom of the stairs. If you slide in quietly, you shouldn't have a problem.

Two guns point at the informer's head.

Only one room left. Take the right passage and open the door out onto the second-story balconies. Everyone here should be dead from earlier. To your left, you can see a large rooftop room. There are two entrances: one to the far left and one straight ahead at the other corner.

Two terrorists train guns on the informer inside. The best approach is to have Price wait on a Zulu command to "open and clear" at the far left door. You run down to the opposite corner and take that door, since the terrorist closer to your door has a better shot at the informer. Give the Zulu command, and as Price opens his door, you open yours and simultaneously shoot the guards.

The three men talking in the first room on the second floor must be dealt with quickly.

Wander upstairs until you come to the door that takes you into a room with a low-running wall. Make sure you're in crouch position so they don't spot you right away. Turn the corner and start blasting. Two men talk close by, and a third hangs out in the far left corner. Gun them down from the cover of the half-wall.

Only a perfect strike will finish off the two terrorist guards before they finish off the informer.

A grenade blast incinerates the two guards from the back room.

Two reinforcements wait in the room behind this one (the two doorways in the back of the room). They'll charge when you hit the halfway point of the room. Instead, fire one of those handy explosive grenades into the right doorway and the terrorists will go up like candles.

If Price didn't make it this far, your only choice is to head to the far door and charge in yourself. Run through the door as if you mean to tackle the first terrorist and gun him down as you dart in front of the informer. Absorb whatever hits the second terrorist fires at the informer and down him fast. Finally, the informer is safe and secure. He can spill the beans to your higher-ups so you can start cracking this organization.

MISSION 8: ALCATRAZ

The government has decided to put you away in Alcatraz. Not so you can rot away in a prison cell, but so you can rescue two hostages. Our old friend Juan Crespo, while on a tour of Alcatraz prison, has been captured by the terrorist group. Unless the ransom is paid—and probably even if it is—the terrorists are going to kill Crespo and his tour guide. Break into the prison and break the hold the terrorists have on Crespo.

Alcatraz hasn't been cleaned in years, so expect a dirty mission.

Guns & Ammo

On this mission take along the GALIL ARM and you won't ever have to worry about running out of ammo. Since you've got at least two big fights inside Alcatraz, the GALIL holds up well with 100-round clips. It doesn't have great range— only a 1.5x scope—but it does hit for 60 damage and fires at a 71 accuracy, so you shouldn't miss targets often.

The GALIL comes with an ammunition drum that holds 100 rounds.

When you aren't wielding the GALIL, try the M203 with high-explosive grenades. There are multiple spots inside the prison where you'll need to clear out a mess of enemies in a hurry. You just don't want to use it near the hostages, but that's why you're also carrying flashbang grenades. For some added firepower, your fourth brings some M34 WP grenades to burn out those tough enemy positions.

Rats in the Sewer

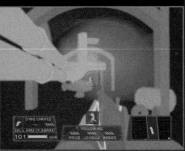

In the sewers, thermal vision can pinpoint bodies, though you'll have to ignore the false readings from steam pipes.

You start your Alcatraz mission in the sewers that run below the complex.

Try to get through as much as you can with s however, it may be impossible. The water you through alerts terrorists of your position, and narrow sewers offer little chance to skirt an e approach from a better angle. Just use the te the best of your ability.

Nail the terrorist in the corner or you'll ha rocket fired at your team.

Walk your way up the first tunnel and look first "roadblock"—a collection of obstacles the use as defensive cover. One terrorist will be s behind the roadblock, with two others in the b corners. You want to eliminate the front terro because he has the best shot on you, but the threat is the terrorist in the back right corner a rocket launcher and is not afraid to use it. I hail bullets at him as soon as the fight starts, least one missile to cruise down the corridor.

At the e tunnel, turn There may enemy wait these steps approach w on the trigg little transit brings you t second mai

Every turn holds a potential enemy.

In the second sewer tunnel, three terrorists have fashioned a makeshift "roadblock."

Much like the first, the second tunnel holds a roadblock too. The terrorists will use the barrels and the alcove as cover. Angle out to the tunnel's right side so you can spot a piece of the hidden guys. Pick off the one in the alcove first, if you have a choice, since his submachine gun can chew through your company if he stays alive long.

At least one terrorist will fall back into the small side tunnel to catch you off guard when you step closer. Eliminate anyone in your way and veer left to tackle that side of the two tunnels running parallel.

Thermals can see enemies hidden behind crates and other objects.

In the side tunnel, you'll spot a stack of crates straight ahead. Don't be fooled—there's a terrorist hiding behind there. If you switch to thermal, you'll see the culprit clear as day. He will lean out from the crates and zing bullets down the tunnel. It's not an easy shot, so train on the spot where he sticks his head out and when he lets loose, you do the same. Your barrage should bring him down before he drops you.

Before you climb the steps up to the prison floor, clear up the terrorists looking to shoot you in the back.

You're almost done with the sewers. At the end of the side tunnel, you have a T-intersection. To the left and up the stairs lies the door to the prison level—your ultimate goal. First, though, two terrorists wait in the shadows to the right. They want you to try those stairs so they can rip into your backs. The plan, however, is to swing quickly around to the right and trigger off several bursts. When they fall, you can ascend the steps and trigger the first waypoint.

Clean Up Act

The shower room sets the scene for the mission's longest firefight. Position your crew carefully or they'll take a thousand bullets.

You're in for a brutal fight in the shower room. It's a big, big room with no apparent exits, little cover, and many hidden terrorists with destructive urges. Superior positioning and combined combat tactics are the only way out.

Set your team off to the right of the door, with their backs flat against the wall. This gives them excellent cover from enemies above them, plus a good shooting angle on the side balconies.

Use night and thermal vision to spot the
terrorists on the upper level.

The terrorists are patient, so you will have to
enter the room and trigger the attacks. Think of
yourself as the guinea pig in an experiment, and
hopefully your team can save your bacon when the
traps spring.

Walk up the left side and stop at the halfway point.
Aim at the balcony in front of you that has no bars. A
terrorist will run out of here and throw an explosive
in your direction if you don't drill him first. This will
trigger a series of attacks, as terrorists detonate
charges around the room to drop mortar and bricks
down on certain locations. You'll be safe if you
proceed to the far end of the room and spin back to
watch the balconies to the right of your team (your
left side). You should now be facing your team.

The bad guys throw explosives at you, so whip out the
grenade launcher and return the favor.

Work in conjunction with your team. If you stay on
this half of the room, you should be well protected on
the right side, but open to fire on your left. You want
to concentrate your attacks on the balconies to the left
and the ones directly above your team. Your team will
spread their fire to the balconies on either side of you,
so you can cover a lot of area. Feel free to sling a few
grenades up into the balconies to pave the way to
peace and quiet.

Terrorists use explosives to charge the room. They also
provide you an avenue of escape.

Eventually, the balconies will be cleared. At this
point, the door to the right of your team (in the corner
to your left) will explode in and a new wave of terrorists
will charge in. This is actually good news. You had no
exit, and they've just provided you with one. The
terrorists will run right by your squad, and the team
should gun them down. If not, the terrorists will charge
right at you, probably looking back at the team who
has opened up on them. The only real danger is you or
your team shooting each other, since you're on
opposite sides of the shower room.

Fight the two terrorists on either side of your new door.

Regroup with the team and head for the new blown-
open door. Don't enter unless you want to get pelted
from both sides. There's a terrorist inside to the left and
one a room away to the right, but still with a clear shot.

In the doorway, angle to your right inch by inch until
you can get a glimpse of the terrorist there. Blow him
away, then jump into the room and fire at the other
enemy through the barred window.

On the upper level, shoot the guards behind the curtain and
continue toward the hostages.

Head up to the balcony level and follow the path to the small room at the end. Two curtained-off areas hold one or two terrorists, depending on who has joined the fight earlier. Spray the area behind the curtains and you should strike flesh and bone. Around the next corner, you'll see a dead civilian on the ground. You've hit the next waypoint, and you get a well-deserved save after a tremendous battle.

Hostage Negotiations

Two terrorists defend the rooms in front of the tour guide.

Head downstairs and wander until you reach the wing with the tour guide. A single terrorist patrols the hallway in front of the tour guide's room. From the doorway, you can frame a perfect shot through the bookcase and take him down with a single burst.

The two terrorists holding the tour guide will sometimes charge out into the fight or stay bunkered to hit you as you open the door.

Hang a right and proceed up the hallway, past the debris. The shaded room in the top left of the map is where the terrorists hold the tour guide. The room below it holds a single terrorist who will join the fight. You want to send your team to "open and clear" the room before the tour guide.

Meanwhile, you wait outside and train your gun on the tour guide's door. If the guards inside hear shooting, they may come out to explore and you have the makings of an easy rescue. If not, flashbang the door and drop the two before the tour guide gets hurt.

You must leave your team temporarily to secure the tour guide while you pursue the terrorists holding Crespo.

For this next step, you're on your own. The boss asks your team to stay behind and safeguard the tour guide, while you look for Crespo. Take the left around behind the tour guide's room and wander down until you reach the cellblock (the big room with lots of little rooms attached to it). There are a bunch of enemies to eliminate. After you engage, your team will double-time to help out.

In the cellblock, fight as many terrorists as you can and wait for your team to reinforce.

Creep into the room and clip the two terrorists up front. Flip back and forth between thermal and normal vision (or night vision if you're having trouble pinpointing an enemy) to find your targets. Two terrorists attack from the top level and two more will find cover at the back of the room. The terrorists particularly like the column in the back right corner. If you move along the right wall, you can pop up into a standing position and blast any enemy reloading there.

Two terrorists will engage you on the upper cellblock level. A third waits behind the far door.

Enemy reinforcements will appear, but so will your team. Together, your firepower will overwhelm the lesser-equipped tangos. When things quiet, take the door to your left, which leads up to the upper cellblock.

At the far end of the upper cellblock, three terrorists will try and stop you. One stands by the column in the far right corner, up on the highest level. The second waits by the window almost directly in front of you as you advance down the cellblock. The third attacks from behind the door at the end of the cellblock. In order from one to three, shoot these enemies and continue on.

Tip

There's nothing worse than rescuing the hostage only to be shot by the last straggling terrorist. Always be sure the area has been mopped up before attending to the hostage.

Stage a two-front attack on Crespo's room. You attack from the upper balcony, while your team performs an "open, flash and clear" maneuver down below.

Wander downstairs and eventually you come to a hallway with a small door to your left and double doors ahead. Crespo is on the other side, along with four terrorists. Give your team a Zulu command to "open, flash and clear" and have them wait as you gain position on the upper level. Climb the stairs behind the left door and set up by one of the barred windows up there. Hit Zulu and, after the room flashes, stand up and start firing down on the terrorists. Make sure you don't hit your teammates as they crash into the room.

Scan for any remaining terrorists hidden in Crespo's room.

The terrorists should be in enough disarray to lose this fight without even thinking about capping Crespo as a going-away present. Watch for any terrorists who still may be up on the upper level (same as you). If anything moves, shoot it.

When all quiet's down, retreat to Crespo's room and give the order to secure the hostage.

Juan Crespo is safe once again.

First you saved Crespo's company and employees. Now you've saved the man himself. If you keep this up, you may have a big inheritance in your future.

MISSION 9: IMPORT/EXPORT

Emilio Vargas, Juan Crespo's right-hand man, looks to be the terrorist culprit. The U.S. and Venezuelan governments can't prove it yet, but it appears as if Vargas has been employing illegal banking practices to create terrorist "slush funds" in the Middle East. Intel has tracked down one of Vargas's business, and they want you and your team to sneak in and recover as much evidence as possible linking Vargas to the terrorist group. If you muck up the works a bit, so much the better.

Your superiors ask you to keep the killing to a minimum, but that's only a guideline, not a rule.

Guns & Ammo

With both outdoor and indoor action, get your hands on an assault rifle. There are many good choices, though for variety we dust off the TAR-21. It has decent numbers across the board, and it holds 30-round clips. You don't want to take any of the 20-round guns on this little trip, since there will be a lot of shooting along the way.

The TAR-21 has good damage and accuracy. It holds 30-round clips, and you'll need every bullet for this mission.

In case of auxiliary help, carry along the 92FS pistol with silencers. You never know when you have to pop someone without the whole neighborhood hearing. Of course, the M203 HE should be standard on any mission you can afford to fit it in. You don't have to rescue any prisoners in this mission, so the smoke grenades are more a distraction than a nonlethal strategy in an area containing civilians.

Bodies of Evidence

 From the starting point, walk around the truck and take the first door to your right. Your superiors ask you to keep the killing to a minimum, but that's out the window as soon as you enter the building. There's an enemy dead ahead, and he fires on you without hesitation. Return fire and blow him to smithereens. Two companions will join

Look for the evidence in the first building near the insertion zone.

him, and you should plaster the wall with them as well. The most dangerous terrorist hides is the right corner. As soon as you open the door, he'll start shooting at you from his position. If you can shoot his three companions from the doorway, you can swing in and take care of him when you have a chance.

Four terrorists intercept you right away.

Walk behind the counter and head right. When you get to the next hallway, turn left and peer down the longer hallway. You should spot a terrorist in the weapons armory. Fire down the corridor until you nip him, then advance on the position.

Press down the hallway, eliminating the defenders along the way, and grab the first set of evidence in the end room.

About three quarters of the way down, another terrorist threat will spring from his room. Prepare to unload as soon as you see motion. Continue toward the armory, going slow to ensure you didn't miss any terrorists who may have retreated to the armory area. When you secure the weapons, you have your first piece of evidence against Vargas.

RAINBOW SIX 3

Dirty Business

Outside again, two rooftop assassins hope to cut you down.

Leave the weapons armory and exit to the outside. You need to head right to the stairs that climb to the second story. Before you can get there, though, two assassins run across the roofs to have their way with you. Give them any amount of time and you're all dead. The one along the gray building will strafe your entire team; the red-shirted one atop the pink building will lob a grenade down into your midst and trigger a clip from the roof corner. Anticipate their attack and knock them off the roofs before too much damage can be inflicted.

Shoot the terrorists before they can gain cover behind the toppled table.

At the top of the stairs, the door opens into a large room with a toppled table in the middle. Four terrorists are spread out in the room. One will be near the door. A second will walk the floor near the table. The third and fourth are in the rooms to your left. After you enter the room, a fifth will charge at you from the door in the far room.

Tip

Don't let any of the terrorists use toppled furniture as cover. They will stay defensive and only expose the hand holding the submachine gun as they spray you blind.

Come in guns blazing. Make sure you move in and slide to the right so the rest of your team can contribute. The doorway is a tight squeeze, so if you blast away from there, it will only be you fighting all the terrorists. Prevent the terrorists from reaching the toppled table and securing cover. If you can keep them exposed in the open, you have an excellent chance of escaping without a wound.

In the TV room, one terrorist stands out in the open, while the second hides behind the toppled table.

Exit the room with the five dead terrorists, cross through a small hallway, and open the door on the other side. You'll see a guard waiting by a TV. Shoot as you enter the room and spread out on the floor. The second terrorist is a bit trickier. He has the protection of a bulky refrigerator to screen him, plus the cover of a toppled table. He likes to duck down and spray the whole room randomly with his submachine gun over the top of the table. Let him fire and when he goes to reload, run to the side of his barricade and plug him square in the chest.

In the next room, shoot the two terrorists with the flashlights and then the one guarding the downstairs.

Open the next door and look for the flashlights. The guards on patrol here use flashlights, which makes for a great target to zero in on. Wipe them out and cross the room to the door in the far left corner. Carefully inch out onto the walkway and look down and to your right. There will be a single terrorist guarding the downstairs. You need to mop him up or else he'll harass your team with gunfire as you navigate the walkways.

If you continue along the pathway, you'll be dead twice. Two assassins have the walkway's window in their sights. You need to slide to your right and expose only the tiniest fraction of your gun as you search for the first assassin. He kneels on the far platform in the warehouse. Blast

Proceed past the windows carefully. You have assassins waiting to pop you through the pane.

through the window and hit with a barrage to knock him off the ledge. Continue on and aim back to your left where the second assassin will no doubt be lining up a shot on you.

Open the corner door and assault the warehouse from the tiny balcony. Shoot the red barrels to set off explosions that will remove chunks of guys.

The door in the corner opens onto a small balcony overlooking the warehouse. Be careful that the warehouse guards don't hit the red barrel in the corner of the balcony. If they do, it will blow the whole area sky high and you'll take a heckuva lot of damage. Of course, you can return the favor. There are two barrels in plain sight: one on the top platform near where the first assassin knelt, and a second down on the floor beneath your balcony.

Caution

The red barrels contain explosive chemicals. Shoot them and the fireworks begin.

When you're ready, charge out on the balcony with your team and fire at the terrorist on the middle platform to your left. Let your team fire around the warehouse as you aim at the red barrel on the ground floor. If you can ignite it, you'll doom all the enemies on the warehouse floor.

When you've finished off the warehouse guards, turn around and look for the next door along the walkway. The terrorists on the other side are a bit impatient and will already have lobbed a grenade to blow the door into itty-bitty

Another outdoor assassin aims at you through the window.

pieces. If they haven't, wait a few seconds and they will. The corridor beyond isn't safe either. They'll throw a second grenade to detonate in the middle. Wait till these explosions are over before attacking.

Gun down the four terrorists in the infirmary.

Sight down the narrow hallway and shoot anyone you might see down there. Most likely, you won't see anyone. They're hiding and hoping you come down after them. However, before you can reach them, you have to deal with another assassin outside the window to your left. Slide to your right and snipe him through the curtain before he turns to bury a bullet in your forehead.

In the infirmary at the end, you have four terrorists to keep track of in the chaos. One or two will be near the main room. A third will search for cover in the adjoining room. The fourth will be to your left behind the extra cots by the telephone. Kill them in rapid succession and take the stairs in the next room.

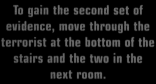

To gain the second set of evidence, move through the terrorist at the bottom of the stairs and the two in the next room.

At the bottom of the stairs, a terrorist waits to surprise you behind the curtain. Slide out and pick him off by aiming at an exposed shoulder or leg. The door beyond opens into a small room with two more terrorists. You can either charge in and gun them down mano-y-mano or issue a "breach and clear" command to your team if you really want to be sure.

The second set of evidence condemning Vargas rests in the office beyond. Enjoy the save point and prepare for a lot of upcoming combat.

Taking Out the Garbage

Cap the first terrorist through the office window, then step outside and zoom in on the upper story window for the second assassin.

Switch to your 92FS in the office and look at the window. There will be a terrorist right there ready to hammer you as you exit into the street. Disrupt his plans with a little assassin job of your own.

Step out and turn to your left. A terrorist will attack you from the window on the far right. Aim for the bottom left pane and squeeze off a burst as soon as his head comes into view. Shoot until you don't see his ugly mug anymore.

Wipe out the three terrorists on the right side of the truck yard.

Head out into the truck yard. There will be three terrorists on your right side, and you should deal with them first since they have the best angle on you. Fire at the one standing out in the open first. After he falls, advance slowly and sight up high on the balcony to your right. An assassin will come into view with a sniper rifle trained on your head. You'll have to be fast to stop him from hitting you at least once. The third tango will lean out from behind the shed around the first corner. Smear him with a burst to the stomach or head.

Track down the final two terrorists in the truck yard.

At this point there are only two more terrorists outside. The first hides behind a stack of pallets and will not jump out until you get close. Zoom on his head at range and drop him before he becomes a threat. The last terrorist can be found behind trucks in the back of the yard. Sometimes he reinforces from the right side, and sometimes he sits back there and waits for you to come to him. You want to eliminate him so he doesn't sneak up on you later when you take on the second warehouse.

The warehouse terrorists come at you in waves. Drop the ones on the ground floor first so they don't return fire.

You must watch three potential spots where the enemy can get the angle on you from above.

When the five outside terrorists are down, cross to the left side and follow the wall until you find a small opening you can enter. There is a bay door that grinds shut as you approach. Bring your men up on the platform and wait for the bay doors to rise again.

Next, glance up at both storage shelves. At least one guard will try and shoot down at you from the very top level. Kill these guys quickly or they'll rain lead down on multiple team members. A third terrorist shoots from the upper window on the back wall. Once you have these elevations cleared, you even the playing field to your level.

Get ready for a big fight. There are a dozen terrorists inside that want a piece of you, and they just might get it if you're not careful. As the doors open, fire on the terrorists in the foreground; they have the best chance of hitting you.

You might think you've cleaned up the warehouse crew, but watch for reinforcements who slip in from the rear.

Fire a few grenades at various points around the warehouse. You'll kill or shake the terrorists into doing something stupid like running to a new position and getting gunned down by your teammates.

However, don't think it's over so easy. When you hear another set of bay doors grinding open, prepare for a rear assault as some of the terrorists double around. They will attack from the same direction you entered.

There will be a lot of carnage when you're done.

Eventually, you'll penetrate the warehouse and slaughter whoever tries to fight back. The mystery game is over for Vargas; you have exposed his operation. He won't be too happy about that, and that's just the way you like it.

MISSION 10: PENTHOUSE

Vargas is on the run. He's smart enough not to use his penthouse home anymore, but he may try and contact someone there. You're going to leave your team behind on this one; it's a solo mission. Get in and bug Vargas's telephone and computer, then wait for further instructions. As always, there will be some other nasty surprises too.

Guns & Ammo

On a solo mission that doesn't rely on firing a single shot, it doesn't matter what weapon you take. The name of this game is stealth. In case you need to fire later on—say, the mission changes, wink, wink—bring along weapons with suppressed fire. The MK23 is your only choice. Should you need to off someone, you can do it quietly without alerting anyone else in the immediate area.

Make a peep or have one guard see you and the mission's over.

You get tear gas and a mask. Unlike other missions, though, you probably won't have a need for them.

Tip

To quickly view the level's opposition, check out the red dots on your in-game minimap—these dots represent all the guards you'll need to avoid.

Bug Out

If you think you hear someone coming, duck into the shadows and hope they pass by without seeing you.

While planting the bugs, you can't be seen. If you do, the mission is blown. That means sticking to the shadows, analyzing the guard patterns and walking very slowly to avoid the slightest bit of noise. Practice your walking in the starting room if you need to get it down to a science.

Take the door in the starting room and wander through till you reach the glass doors. Notice that there's a glass ceiling above. If you happen to pass beneath it at the same time as a guard walks on it above—bang—you're nailed. You may want

Near the second set of doors, there's a glass ceiling. Be careful of patrolling guards passing overhead.

to wait until you see the guard walk by overhead, then slip through the glass doors.

Tip

You don't have to worry about closing doors in the house. The guards won't notice that previously closed doors have now mysteriously opened.

In a delicate maneuver, you must walk by two guards simultaneously.

Practice your real slow walk to slip by the guard watching TV.

At the intersection, turn right and walk until you can see the living room. The guard watches TV with his back to you. If you walk very slowly you can pass behind him, through the kitchen, and up the stairs without attracting any attention. One inadvertent slip into a run and he turns to see what the noise is. You can't shoot even a silenced bullet into the back of his head, so the walk is your only option.

Walk into the side room and bug the telephone.

At the top of the stairs continue straight. Twenty feet away, the telephone beckons for you. Don't succumb and make a break for it. Any running inside will attract attention. You must be patient and walk down the hall and into the telephone room. The phone lies around the corner to your right. Hold the action button, and when the action circle completes, you have one tapped phone.

Your next task is to tap the computer. Just down the hallway, it should be a breeze, right? You know the answer better than I do: No chance. Two guards patrol the area and you have to cut between both of them.

Leave via the opposite door in the telephone room. Step out into the main hallway and notice that a wall divides the hallway most of the way. To the right, a lone guard walks through several rooms and then down the hall directly at your current position. To the left—the hallway section with the glass floor that you previously passed under—another guard watches the stairs up to the third floor.

The accountant works on the main computer, so you have to go to plan B.

When the right guard comes into view, sidestep to the left side and begin walking. Go slow and steady and the left guard won't turn around. You have just enough time to reach the far side of the corridor before the right guard turns into the area you just walked through.

Head straight ahead toward the glass double doors. That was your original target, but things have changed. An accountant hacks away at the computer, so you must switch to the backup target—a laptop computer in the master bedroom upstairs.

Step out from behind the divider. You will have to deal with two terrorists around the bedroom area. The guard patrolling the hallway may already be inside the room, so prepare to fire. A second guard may be in the bathroom straight ahead, so watch for that door opening. If you only down one terrorist in the bedroom, the other one will be out in the hallway looking to stop you before you get started.

Move upstairs to the secondary computer in the master bedroom. Wait for the bedroom guard to leave before entering.

Continue past the computer room and up the stairs to the third floor. Eventually, you will make a left in the upstairs hallway and take the corner door, but first you have to wait for the bedroom guard to leave. If you get up there too quickly, he'll be in the act of searching the bedroom and you'll never make it past him.

As soon as he leaves, walk into the bedroom and find the laptop on the right side behind a divider. Plant the bug the same way you did on the telephone to complete your bug objectives.

Enter the computer room and shoot the single terrorist before he pops the accountant.

Creative Accounting

You're now free to fire at the guards.

Things change up now. The bug you planted on the telephone pays off immediately. Vargas has contacted his men to eliminate the accountant. Apparently, the accountant knows too much, which makes him the perfect informant. Your new objective is to rescue the accountant, and you get to use weaponry this time.

Tip

The computer room's glass doors are bulletproof. You can't shoot through them.

After you've finished off the two bedroom guards, head down the same stairs you came up and attack the computer room. You can't shoot through the glass doors, so open them quickly while the terrorist's back is still to you. Peg him before he can shoot you or the helpless accountant.

Make sure the accountant follows you before you head for the extraction zone.

Secure the accountant and have him follow you. Don't walk out of the room until you make sure the accountant is indeed walking behind you. He's slow enough as it is, but if he gets lost or stays behind, consider him a cooked goose.

No More Mr. Nice Guy

Nail the terrorists just outside the computer room.

Remember all those guards you had to slip past without so much as a breath. Forget about it now. You can fire at will. There will be at least two terrorists outside in the hall by the computer room, so finish them off with a volley of hushed bullets.

Retrace your steps to the telephone room, since you know the path so well by now. On the way, blast the guard by the stairs and watch for that second guard who may be close by on his patrol.

Retrace your steps and pick off the guard by the stairs.

Three terrorists will set up in the living room area as a last line of defense. You can assault them from the telephone room's doorway, or you could also work your way to the back entrance into the kitchen and attack from there. If you know where they are, either approach works.

The main contingent of guards waits in the living room and kitchen for your return.

The first guard hides at the bottom of the stairs. The second crouches down by the kitchen cabinets, while the third is the original guard watching TV. He has all his attention on the battle at hand now.

Fire on the guard at the bottom of the stairs. You don't want him charging up and getting off a point-blank shot. Next, swing out and shoot down on the TV guard. He has a good angle on you if you don't take care of him from the doorway. Lastly, scan for the guard in the kitchen area and snipe him while moving toward the stairs.

You can alternately sneak around to the kitchen's back door and mow down the guards from there.

Escort the accountant to the extraction zone.

There are other guards in the building, but if you hurry, you won't have to face any more on your way to the extraction zone. Ideally, you want to keep the fighting

to a minimum and cut down on the risk of the accountant turning into Swiss cheese. Navigate back through the starting point and up the stairs to the extraction zone on the roof. The two guards will engage you either on the stairs or on the rooftop. Open the door and shoot to your left to down the first terrorist, then look out by the chairs or by the skylights for the second one. With another informant in tow, you now have everything you need to crack this Vargas terrorist organization wide open.

MISSION II: MEAT PACKING PLANT

The nerve of those terrorists. Vargas's organization has been stockpiling VX nerve gas at a meat packing plant in Caracas, Venezuela. Though enemies have overrun the complex, there are still some innocents trapped inside; it's up to you to retrieve them safely. While you're penetrating the compound, seize as much of the VX as possible. Should this deadly stuff actually see use, we're talking major catastrophe.

All looks peaceful at the meat packing plant. Don't be deceived.

Guns & Ammo

Why not take the best submachine gun with you on your trip into the confines of a meat packing plant? The MP5A4 spits out 30-round clips at a damage of 21 and an accuracy of 44. Compared to the other submachine guns, it packs a punch—only the SR-2 and UMP reach the 20-damage threshold too—and its 3.5x zoom gives you lots of options in larger spaces.

The MP5A4 has the best range and damage of any submachine gun.

Since you're heading into a possible VX situation, the gas mask is a must. You don't want to get caught inhaling toxic gases at any point. Combine the M203 CS with the gas mask, so you can launch tear gas at your enemies without succumbing to the acrid smoke yourself. A few spare flashbang grenades round out your arsenal in case you need them to neutralize hostage rooms.

Dead Meat

Enter the building and you'll run into the first

You start outside in a beautiful, peaceful courtyar Looking in all directions, there's no one to bother but that's all about to change once you move insi After wandering for a bit, you should find the doo hidden behind the shed-like covering, and you hav use the steps on the side.

Your first room has no resistance. It's a bi corral area where, presumably, the cows are before they're butchered. Or maybe it's just a shaped obstacle course? Either way, hang a r the door and follow it straight down to the do the end. You'll pass by a door on your right; t for a bit later.

The fireworks in the first packing room will ignite as s you pop the guard in the control room.

Open the door and look right. A single guard patrols this hallway, which has an impassable barricade about three quarters of the way up. Depending on what point in the guard's route yo open the door, the guard could have his back to or he could be facing you ready to have at it. Sh him from the doorway before he can line up a b shot. It's better to eliminate him now with this relatively easy shot than to let him reinforce late

Eliminate the terrorists inside the packing room and then move to the compartment behind the bay door.

Return to the door you passed in the corral area. ... opens on the first meat-packing room, though it's ...ke a scene from a horror movie. Inside, you have a ...fferent kind of butcher, as the terrorists wander ...round in gas masks looking to do who knows ...hat with cow flesh and VX toxin.

The first guard walks back and forth in the ...ontrol room directly in front of your door. If you wait ...ntil he approaches the glass window, his head ...hould be fully exposed for a big fat target. As soon ...s you down him, the real fireworks start.

After you trigger your first shots or one of the ...uards spots you, the back bay door opens and the ...ther four terrorists (not counting the control room ...uard) fan out into the room. One heads to a ...anister northwest of your position. Two more fire ...rom the protection of the bay door area. The fourth ...ides along the control room wall (you won't be able ...o see him from the doorway area). Shoot the two ...ar guards since they should be right there in your ...ne of sight. As they fall, swing over and zoom on ...he guard hiding by the barrels. He dies if you can ...nd a good shot through the obstructions.

Tip

Listen to the sounds of combat. When an enemy ceases fire, it usually means he's reloading or can't see you. That's the time to pounce.

Reload and go after the last terrorist. He will shoot ...s soon as you cross past the control room corner and ...ead up toward the bay doors. Slide out to your left and ...re a quick barrage at him, then duck back behind the ...afety of the corner. You can repeat as often as you like

Gather your team in the bay door area and you'll get the first mission objective message. Open the nearby door and ready for a terrorist in the hallway (usually in front of the door or off to the right). Plug him and move on.

Plaster the single guard in the corridor between packing rooms.

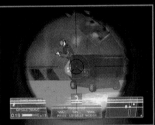

The ambush comes from behind the curtain, but the most pressing danger is the terrorist behind the Dumpster in the rear.

The second packing room lies behind the door to your right and will test your 360-degree vision. The enemy has an ambush planned; to beat it, you'll have to be fast on the trigger finger.

The setup works like this. Inside in the back corner of the room (to your right as you enter), a single terrorist waits behind a Dumpster for the perfect opportunity to rip into the backs of multiple targets. At the same time, across the room, a swarm of terrorists will charge out of the curtained back room. One will run along the walkway on the far side, firing the whole way as he tries to meet up with the Dumpster terrorist. Another will cross to your side of the room and try to flank you in the opposite corner. The rest will use the hanging meat as cover.

Fire at all the swarming terrorists and use the hanging meat
...

How do you survive the overrun? Barge into the room and turn toward the Dumpster enemy. You must eliminate him in the first second or he will gun down you or at least one of your companions. Kill him and turn and take out the terrorist running along the walkway. Let your team fire at the others as you move to the nearest meat slab or the walkway, whichever gets you the best angle on the remaining terrorists. There's no way to avoid wounds in this fight—unless you get extremely lucky—but if you act fast enough you can prevent a really bad scene.

If you aren't careful, the strategically placed resistance in the first hostage room will do you in.

With the ambush over, regroup through the curtains in the side room

the terrorists began in. Follow through the doors until you see the long room with a stack of crates in front of you, barrels to your left and rows of tables beyond. This is the first hostage room, and you have five terrorists to account for—then and only then can you release the hostage.

Even when you think the coast is clear, there are still one or two more terrorists lingering around.

The first terrorist lingers by the barrels to your left. If you open the door and slide in just a hair, he probably won't see you. Shoot him down so he can't return fire. If he does, it can rip into your whole team.

Move into the room and use the crates as cover. You can view the left half of the room, and that's good since three other terrorists are there. The closest will be in the center of the tables and can be brought down with a neck or headshot. The second terrorist will be somewhere in the rear, usually in the back left corner by the barrel. The third terrorist peers out at the room from the high, horizontal window. Zoom on either the second or third terrorist, whoever you think poses the greatest threat.

Twenty terrorists later and you have one freed hostage.

When those three are down, advance into the room. Watch the doorways on the right side. One terrorist remains, and he will try to catch you off guard as you cross. Prepared, you should catch him first. Finally, you can proceed to the back door and the room with the horizontal window. Free the hostage.

Traps Within Traps

In the small warehouse, one acrobatic terrorist will try and lure you into an ambush.

From the first hostage room, continue through the door until you reach the small warehouse. You'll see the stacks of boxes and a catwalk high overhead in the room's rear. As soon as you enter the room and can see between the stacked boxes, a terrorist will leap from the left and roll out of sight to the right. He hopes that you will follow him into the ambush ahead.

The third ambush terrorist throws a grenade down on your position before pouring it on with machine gun fire.

Look around the stacked boxes and you'll see a large hangar door half open. The acrobatic terrorist hides on the other side and will fire when you get close. Also, a second terrorist aims at your position from the catwalk along the back wall. Shoot him first if you can get a good angle without exposing yourself. Next, slide out toward the big door and try and clip the acrobatic guard before you enter his area of fire.

You're not out of the woods yet. A third terrorist—the most dangerous one—also patrols the catwalk. Unlike his fellow assassin, he will not engage in a gun battle. Instead, as soon as you cross into the second half of the warehouse, he will pull the pin on a grenade and throw it right down on your head. To get past him, you must dart into the area, make him throw the frag, then dart back around the big door for protection. After the detonation, sight up on the catwalk and take him down.

Three terrorists defend the cafeteria.

Next stop, the cafeteria and three armed men you won't be sitting down to tea with. Enter from the rightmost doors and you should see in front of you a big column dividing the center of the room. Off to your left, one guard readies his weapon at the vending machines. You can challenge him from this position without risking return fire from the others. Make sure that snack he just ate is his last.

You have two left. One of them hides on the opposite side of the column, while the second uses one of the corners in the back of the room as cover. Slide out to

your left a bit so you can get the angle on the second terrorist and coax him to stain the carpet. Continue sliding out to the left until you can line up the last terrorist by the column. If you're having trouble, you can send your team one way as a distraction while you jump around the other and catch him in the back.

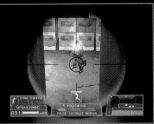

Terrorists converge while you try to open the locked door.

The steps outside the cafeteria lead up to the warehouse catwalk where the terrorists staged the ambush against you. Well, those cunning bad guys have another trick up their sleeves. It's another trap, but with your positions swapped. When you try and pick the door lock at the end of the catwalk, terrorists will pour in from the big door that you just crossed through minutes before. Three or four of the terrorists will fire at you from down below, while one or two will rush through the cafeteria to come up behind you on the catwalk.

Set your team to fire down on the lower warehouse *before* you attempt to pick the lock. Let them do most of the dirty work, but they will be distracted by the mess below. From the corner, you will have to stand out of your crouch and aim over your companions' head down the catwalk. As soon as the terrorists climb those steps, you must gun them down or your teammates are in trouble.

Through the locked door, enter the hallway and then open the door into the office. Through the wide office window, you can actually see the hostage on his knees and the terrorist standing next to him. Since you have the time, aim for a headshot and squeeze the trigger.

Shoot the terrorist holding the hostage at gunpoint through the window.

Another terrorist waits to the right of the door, while several more run around below.

A well-executed shot will remove the immediate threat to the hostage. Still, there is another terrorist to the right of the door and a couple down below on the floor. Open the door and blow away the guard on the walkway, then send your team out onto the catwalk to unload on the terrorists below. A few seconds later and you'll be sending the hostage home.

Freezer Burn

Blast a set of terrorists at each first-floor door in the second hostage room.

Head down to the lower level beneath the hostage. Behind the double doors midway along the wall, two terrorists wait for an ambush possibility. Give your squad a "breach and clear" command on the doors. The terrorists won't survive the blast and subsequent clearing. Outside the doors on your right, two more terrorists will try and throw up some resistance. You can "breach and clear" here or cut them down yourself—whatever will cause potentially less damage to the team.

Click on thermal vision in the freezer to put your foes on ice.

Just ahead you have the freezer. Switch to thermal and study the room from the open doorway. Two guards patrol the top catwalk, while four others man the ground floor (two on either side of you). If you stay in the doorway, the ground terrorists cannot charge you, since the rows of beef are in their way. Use this to your advantage and wait until you have clear shots at each catwalk terrorist. To eliminate the four ground terrorists, shift back and forth near the doorway to line up shots under the carcasses and between the crates.

Travel through the smaller freezer to reach the room where the VX is stored.

In the back left corner, open the freezer door and wander through the smaller freezer to the exterior of the large warehouse. You have two entrances, the double doors to your right and the single door up a bit on your left. Use the single door; it gives you a stack of boxes that shields you from half the terrorists.

Scan the main floor and upper balcony for targets.

You will attack the warehouse in three steps. Step one has you snipe from the doorway. First zoom on the terrorist on the walkway directly across from you. Hit him square and then swing up to your left where you can blast the two terrorists up on the balcony. Make sure they drop or your whole team will pay when you move to the second step. Before that, though, kill the fourth terrorist on the ground floor near the warehouse's center.

As you move out into the warehouse, look to the rear near the bay doors for more terrorists.

For step two, slide out to your right and bring the rest of your team in. As you slide out, more of your team will become involved in the fight. Provide a steady stream of cover fire as your men take position. Once all four of your rifles start firing, the terrorists have no chance. Be careful that a few terrorists don't dig themselves in behind the boxes in the back and surprise you later.

When you dismantle the first terrorist wave, a second wave will arrive through the bay doors.

The terrorists will eventually reinforce as the back bay doors open. You should have a nice perimeter for the upcoming battle. Leave your team to fire at will and angle out to pick off any troublesome terrorists.

That's not oil in those drums. Secure the VX materials before the terrorists figure out how to use the stuff.

They will all drop before your clips come up empty. Take your whole team into the room behind the bay doors and have them fan out to check one last time for stragglers. The VX canisters are in the back right corner. You've scored a major stash and saved thousands of lives by condemning these poisons to the nearest toxic waste dump.

MISSION 12: GARAGE

Intelligence has tracked down Vargas. The terrorist leader has smuggled the VX into New Orleans through an ingenious method—the toxins have been placed in car radiators. A cargo ship unloaded the cars, and they were trucked over to a garage controlled by Vargas. Both Vargas and the VX canisters are now at this garage. No time to waste, you and Loiselle have a lot of ground to cover in the next few hours.

A lot of fancy cars are going to be shot to pieces on this mission.

Guns & Ammo

The M16A2 has everything you need for this mission. Its 30-round clips should last you through the series of garage fights, plus its 66 damage should floor terrorists definitely. You don't want to mess around with only two on your team this time around. Missing isn't much of an option with the M16A2's 74 accuracy and 3.5x zoom.

The M16A2 makes a return appearance to put an end to Vargas once and for all.

Knowing there will be some fierce fighting ahead, arm yourself with the M203 HE to clear rooms and some additional frags, just in case you run low. Leave home without a gas mask and you may not report in for the next mission.

Gas Mileage

Shoot the guards on the showroom floor first.

You've been on Vargas's trail for a few missions. Now you get to hunt him down. Chase Vargas through his

garage and shut down his VX operation. If you're to slow, Vargas will escape and you'll be left spinning your wheels.

But first you have to wade through all of Vargas's men. You begin with the showroom after you open the outer main doors. Two guards walk the floor, the cars the cover between you. Hold your shot on the first on until you can spot both of them. You want these two of the way because they are the only ones who can g a good shot off against you while you're in the doorwa

After the immediate threats are down, look to the offic and the balcony for reinforcements.

Another enemy will attack from the corner office. I you down the first two like clockwork, you may have a shot at the office terrorist through his window. Shoulc the door open, sight on the doorway and pop the assailant as he exits. You don't want him to reach the showroom floor or you have the same situation as the first two terrorists.

To your left, a balcony runs along the second half o the showroom about 15 feet above the ground floor. U on this balcony, several terrorists will rush back and forth between the wall that you can see from the doorway and the stairs around the corner to your left Usually, you will have one planted just out of sight arou the corner, another past the L-bend and a third at the top of the stairs. The enemy on the stairs can still fire

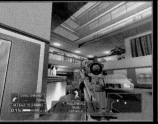

Advance on the stairs to the second level and cut down the resistance.

Angle out to your right and snipe each terrorist that comes into view. Try and get Loiselle out far enough so that his weapon becomes a factor. Do your job right and you can isolate on the balcony guards without worrying about anyone on the lower level.

Advance on the stairs when you eliminate the upper level defense. But have you wiped out everyone? When you come up on the balcony level, a lone gunman aims down on you from the third level. Glance up above where the hanging yellow sign connects to the third level. The assassin will pop up there and shoot to kill. Zoom with the M16A2's 3.5x scope and nail him when he's not suspecting it.

High up on the third level, a lone assassin hopes to catch you unaware.

Caution

You can't reach the third level by foot, but that doesn't mean an enemy assassin can't be placed up there.

Head downstairs to the garage level and erase the first three guards.

Wind through the conference room and look for the stairs on the other side. At the bottom, a terrorist zings shots up at you. You have two choices: slide out and trigger a burst to silence the enemy or bounce a grenade down the steps and splatter him like a tomato in a blender.

A pair of guards flank the doorway at the bottom of the stairs. You have to pull a smooth maneuver to continue without a scratch. Dart out into the hall, aiming left to plaster the guard in the corner. Continue moving forward so the guard on the opposite side can't get a lock on you (in fact, he may shoot straight across and hit the other guard). As you hit the far wall, keep swinging to your left so you're now facing the opposite direction and barrage the second guard. When the smoke clears, you'll be the only one standing.

Three more terrorists try to intercept you at the blue car.

Continue to the next area that holds three terrorists around a blue car. Shoot one from the hall, and in the ensuing confusion, move in and intercept the other two as they race for cover. From the front of the car, you can hit almost any spot in the area.

Rely on the M16A2's scope to peg threats at range.

Take advantage of the next doorway. It gives you a long view of the corridor running alongside the repair shop. Three enemies guard the way. Hit the headman as he wanders in your direction. The other two will hang back, one crouching to shoot you as you approach and the other using the wall as cover. Your weapon's scope again comes in handy as you can focus on both without falling into their range.

Brush back the terrorist under the hydraulic lift
and the other one in the office.

Move in and take on the remaining terrorists. One of the more aggressive enemies likes to creep up and hide under the hydraulic lift under the red car. Show no mercy on him, since you must clear that area to position yourself against anyone still living. From under the hydraulic lift, you should spot the terrorist in the back office. Blast him through the window so you don't wander through his firing arc.

Kill Vargas's bodyguard, but not the man himself. You need
him alive for questioning.

In the corridor beyond the repair shop, you have to be very careful. You don't want Vargas dead, so be very sure of each shot here. Usually Vargas's bodyguard shows up first (armed and wearing a black suit). When you're sure, take him out. Vargas should be alone now, but as you approach you trigger the next waypoint and Vargas runs for his life.

Vargas wears a purple suit. Shoot him and he won't give up his secrets, which your superiors desperately need.

Closed for Repairs

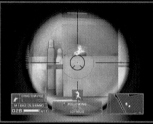

Several of Vargas's men stay behind
to stop you from pursuing.

Vargas leads you into an ambush. Four terrorists hold a wall that Vargas runs by, with two others hoping to lodge some bullets in your chest from across the room. You want the four-man team first. Pop the two guards you can see peeking over the wall. Their backups should try to replace them, in which case you have two more headshots to perform. If not, you'll need to flank them by moving into the room past the wall, but not until you deal with the fifth terrorist.

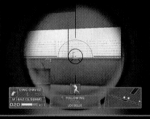

When you round the corner, watch for the office terrorist
and the one hidden in the shadows to your right.

The fifth terrorist slips out of the corner shadows when he sees you. Run into the room without a plan and you won't collect another paycheck. You may want to switch to thermal or night vision to better pick him up. Unfortunately, due to the wall shielding part of his body, you will expose yourself briefly before you can catch enough of his body to bring him down.

The sixth terrorist will shove his weapon through the window for an open attempt to machine gun you once you cross into the room. Pass by the wall and clean up any leftover terrorists, and with the wall as cover, line up the best shot you can on the window guard.

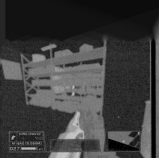

To continue the hunt for Vargas, switch to thermal and hit the next terrorist through a gap in the shelves.

Before you hit the next room, click to thermal so that you can spot the single guard in the next room right away. There are a bunch of shelves that can throw off your shot, and the guard likes to fire right away, so use the thermal vision to pinpoint the flesh-and-blood target between the gaps in the shelves. No one else stands between you and the final room.

When you see the last room, study the right side just prior to where Vargas headed. It's a small coffee area, except it contains a guard who has his back to the wall and finger on the trigger. Slide into view only long enough to spatter the back wall with a new paint scheme.

Before you get to Vargas' last refuge, you must deal with the guard in the coffee room.

Charge into the final room and cut down the guard on the left or you'll eat a hand grenade.

Only one room left, but you can't take it slow like you've done in the past. Vargas makes a break for it as soon as he sees you.

If you're too slow, Vargas will escape down the back corridor to a waiting getaway car.

You've got to be a little wild. Burst around the corner and run full speed toward the doorway on the other side of the room. You have two bodyguards to either side of Vargas. You must, without a doubt, shoot the guard on your left. He holds a grenade and will throw it a split second after you turn the corner. The subsequent blast will rip you to shreds. Shoot him, even if it means getting shot by the second bodyguard. If you have time, turn and shoot back at the right bodyguard. Hopefully, though, Loiselle will pull his weight and chip in on that guard.

Your hot pursuit has paid off and you've nabbed Vargas before he could release the VX gas.

Don't stop running until you have Vargas. If he reaches the back corridor and escapes out into the alley, you fail. You'll hear his car burn rubber and get away. Now wouldn't you rather hear Vargas beg for mercy and spill his guts?

Tip

You can't take it slow in the final room. Either you blaze in and grab Vargas, or he slips through your fingers.

MISSION 13: PARADE

The mastermind behind the terrorists isn't Vargas. It's the guy you've saved twice already—Juan Crespo. He's been right under our noses the whole time, but now the evidence is out to bring him in. The problem is Crespo has his master plan in motion. He plans to blow up a bomb in a parade float in New Orleans and spread VX gas as far as the wind will spread it. Failure is not an option. Stop this terrorist act before it becomes a nightmare.

Stick to the shadows as long as you can to penetrate Crespo's forces.

Guns & Ammo

Our friend the G3A3 is back. What's not to like about the stats? With a 49 range, 87 damage, 65 accuracy, and 3.5x zoom, you're holding arguably the best assault rifle in the game. Its only downside is a slightly smaller ammo capacity with 20-round clips.

You can't go wrong with the G3A3 and its awesome capabilities.

For backup, load your high explosives into the M203. The last half of the mission, you'll be running solo and will need the extra artillery for tight spots. The M34 WP offers the same option, while the smoke grenade can prove a useful defensive screen against big enemy numbers.

Bomb Squad

Note the terrorist's shadow and trace him back to his hideaway.

You begin in almost pitch-black darkness in the back of an alley. All things considered, it's not a bad place to

Crespo's men, and they will have trouble tracking you while you hunt for the bomb.

When you turn the corner and approach the first streetlight, notice the terrorist's shadow to your left. He patrols that side alley and won't walk out into view. Instead, he'll hope that you engage with his friends in the next area and he can pounce on you from behind. Get him out of the way by spinning the corner and blasting him, whether the terrorist is at point-blank range or ducking behind the cover at the back of the alley.

Knock out the terrorists you can see from the alley first. That way you keep the walls as cover for a longer period of time.

As soon as the shooting kicks off, the guards in the shed area (straight ahead from the main alley) will move into position. One will cut across the main alley and drop down behind some barrels in the top left corner. He must be eliminated pronto, otherwise he has a straight shot at everyone in your team.

Two more terrorists will move up and gain cover by the sheds. The first runs up to the cover to your immediate right as you enter the area. The second slips up behind the middle shed. Bring your team up to the opening into the shed area and give them a chance to fire at the incoming terrorists. You should move toward the downed terrorist in the left corner. On the way, unload on the terrorist to the immediate right and try and help flush him out so your teammates can clean up. The middle shed guard will fall if you flank him from the side, and you will if you advance a couple of feet past the

Slip behind the middle shed to flank the remaining alley terrorists.

The remainder of the terrorists reinforce from the rear, emerging out from the square alcove that has the locked door you'll venture to next. Try to shoot as many as you can through the gaps between buildings. You want to keep them pinned back there so they can't gain cover. If you're having trouble flushing the last of them out, bring your team up the right side to angle shots into the alcove, while you advance up the left side and cut down anyone trying to flee.

It's a trap! Three sharp-shooters stare down at you from the rooftops by the locked door.

When there's nothing left but dead bodies, continue to the door in the alcove. It's locked and takes several seconds to pick. You should be suspicious by now, and yes, it's a trap. Three sharpshooters on the rooftops try to puncture as many of you as possible while you're out in the open.

From the locked door, the terrorists are positioned as follows: two on the roof to your right, one at the corner of the two buildings to your left. If you want to be aggressive, the smart thing to do *before* you open the door is set up your team facing the two terrorists on the right-hand roof. That way, when you trigger the trap, you can let your team handle those two while you forget about the door for a second and concentrate on downing the last sniper to your left.

If you'd rather go defensive, send your team deep into the alcove where they will be protected by the overhang. You will either have to battle the three assassins yourself, or try and pick the door and race through the opening before you absorb too much damage. Unless you're really low on health at this point—hopefully not, since you just started—it's better to fight it out.

The terrorist on the stairs drops a grenade and then retreats to fire at you from the upstairs corner.

Inside the locked door, there's a stairwell going up. Don't charge up these stairs or you'll be in for a world of hurt. A lone guard pops the pin on a fragmentation grenade and rolls it down the stairs before retreating. As long as you stay on the bottom flight or floor, you won't take much, if any, damage. Anyone on the first platform or second flight of stairs will be obliterated.

After the explosion, chase after the dastardly terrorist. He will try and inflict further harm from the first corner, as he peeks around and triggers blind bursts from his submachine gun. When he bobs his head out, take it off.

Shoot through the door for one kill, then wrap around the wall for the second.

Open the nearby door and look for another terrorist in the distance through the next open doorway. You should be able to shoot through the adjacent corridor and plink him before he even notices movement. Head into the corridor and look to your left. A second terrorist has retreated into this room, but he's in a really tough spot—in the corner to your immediate left, with a perfect shot at the doorway. You'll have to rush in and take your lumps as you dish out some hot lead.

Overpower the two terrorists in the next hall, then sneak up on the two rooftop guards.

Open the next door in a new hallway and you should see two guards staking out the corner. Unless they've heard you making a racket earlier, they will be facing the opposite direction. Good news for you, since two well-placed bursts will put an end to their threat.

Continue down the long corridor, but watch out for the open doorway on the left-hand side. It leads out onto the roof where another sniper squats at the far end. He will cap the first person to pass the doorway, which usually will be you. Turn and face the wall in front of the door and sidestep until you can fire with the doorway as partial cover. When he falls, don't charge out looking for more action. Another terrorist sits up on the ledge above the door and will drive you into the ground if you walk out more than 10 feet. Instead, take two steps in and train your gun directly above you. You should have a point-blank shot at the last rooftop terrorist.

One stairwell guard prevents you from finding the parade float.

At the end of the corridor, take the stairs down to the outside plaza that holds the float—and the bomb you've been looking for. Only one man stands in your way on the stairs, but the terrorist won't go down easy. He likes to start shooting before you round the corner on him, so you may walk into his gunfire if you don't plan accordingly. If you have a spare grenade, drop it over the side and let the shrapnel do your dirty business. If not, don't rush down the stairs like a crazy man. Inch along the inner wall and when you hear his gunfire, stop. At a pause in the action, slip around the corner and aim for his torso or head to finally bring him down.

Be on your toes against foes in high windows or hidden in parked vehicles.

The door opens on a big plaza with the float in the middle. The bomb has been planted on the right side of the float. Before you can reach there, however, you have several vans and windows to scan over. If you go to thermal, you'll see people inside the vans—a sure tip-off that enemies could swarm at any time. Also, as soon as you approach the float, snipers will attack from the building facing you across the plaza and the one off to the right. Your team might return fire effectively, but you should hit thermals and scope out the windows for potential threats before they engage.

After you deal with the few terrorists surrounding the bomb, call for a "demo up" and shut down that bomb. It seems to work at first, then you realize the stupid thing has a remote backup. While you leave your team to guard the actual bomb, you must go

Deactivate the bomb and leave your team behind as an insurance policy.

solo to hunt for the deadly device. You only have five minutes to save New Orleans.

Race Against Time

If you think you have time, clean out the terrorists in the front section of the hotel so they can't reinforce.

You can do a lot in five minutes, but can you stop a bomb from destroying a city? You're about to find out. From the bomb squad, run along the left side of the hotel and look for a side alley. If you think you have time, you can stop in the hotel's front entrance and battle the bad guys there: two in the main lobby to either side of the door, and the last one behind the bar as you head through the door to your left. This cuts down on reinforcements later, but slows you down earlier. Unless you have the route down to an exact science, skip the main entrance and head straight to the alley.

Turn right into the side alley and look for the door along the right-hand wall. It's the backdoor into the pool hall, and the guards won't expect you that way.

You have five minutes to find the remote detonator or the bomb's still going up along with your team.

You have three tangos to shoot in rapid succession if you don't want any counterattacks. The first one will bend down and use the pool table to your left as cover. Even so, he'll still leave his upper torso, neck, and head exposed for a clutch shot. The guard in the right corner aims for you as you aim for the left guard. Trigger off an accurate burst on the left guard, and you'll have just enough time to swing and catch the right guard before he lets loose. The middle guard stands in the doorway between the two pool halls and is the slowest of the bunch. Even with two separate fights before you get to him, you will still nail him before he manages to drill you.

Shoot the guards in the pool hall before they see you in the doorway.

One of the terrorists will drop a smoke grenade in between the two rooms at this time. Great. Switch to thermal vision and you can see through the gray smoke, while they can't. Advance on the room, but watch your right for the first doorway. The bartender has a present for you should you take a few more steps. Instead, smear him as soon as his heat signature appears. You have time; the smoke shields you, and if one of the other terrorists advances, prioritize him instead of advancing.

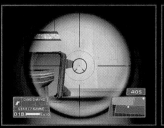

A terrorist drops a smoke grenade, and that's a big plus for you. Switch to thermal so you can see while the terrorists can't.

The terrorists in the back of the pool hall won't be fooled. Fortunately, the smoke should still be thick and allow you to sneak up closer. To your left will be a sniper and another assault rifle-toting thug to your right. Spray a healthy dose of ammo at the sniper and drag it across to the right terrorist. Attack any terrorists who may still be active while the smoke still provides some cover.

When you think you've got them all, weave through the pool tables to the door on your left. Half the time, you may find one last terrorist hidden in the corner to the left of the door. Be sure that your weapon is quicker than his.

Shoot the terrorists in the back of the pool hall so you can reach the stairs.

Climb the stairs to the second story and stop on the platform before the floor. You should see two terrorists behind a barricade; they make easy targets from the shadows of the stairs. To your right, notice a weird gated area, right before the second floor landing. A single terrorist waits in here, and his first inclination will be to pull the pin on a grenade and make you eat it. Sidestep in front of this gate and trigger off several bursts to make sure he's dead and can't get off that grenade.

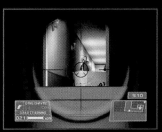

Pop the two terrorists at the top of the stairs, but don't forget about the hidden terrorist in the cage.

Veer to your right and survey the terrace area. One terrorist crouches directly ahead of you. A second one will come out of the room down the hall to the left when you start shooting. Sight on the first guard and bring him down with an accurate shot. Quickly move ahead so that the big column at the corner hides you from the room the second terrorist leaves. He won't know where you are, and you'll be able to slip out and zap him when he's not looking.

On the second floor, zing the two nearby terrorists then look to the balcony overhead to prevent a lobotomy.

Continue down this side of the terrace until about the halfway point. Point your gun up at the next level and inch forward until you can pinpoint the corner closest to you. A terrorist sniper will gradually emerge into view. Smash him back, or he'll kill you while you try to cross to the other side.

Fire on the last second-level guard and clip more snipers up top.

Your goal is the opposite corner where a hallway leads to the third-floor staircase. Shoot the guard in that hallway, and as you cross over to the second walkway, watch the balcony above again for two more snipers. If the one before was bad, two is worse, so be careful.

At the corners, two terrorists present easy targets.

In the next hallway, run till you hit the stairs on your right. More terrorists will try and slow you down, but you can run right past them. At this point, you'll be low on time and won't want to engage them.

Wind your way up to the third level and shoot the guard straight down the hallway. Turn left and shoot the second guard at the corner of the terrace area.

Advancing on the terrace, which you have to do, will trigger a large attack. Two terrorists will fire at you from the superior position above the glass ceiling, while another will flank you to the left. Use the corner column as protection from the guard to your left and unload an entire clip if you have to and bring down the two terrorists above. Slide out to the right and kill the last terrorist when you see the opportunity.

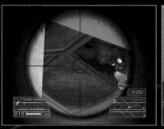 

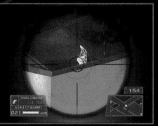

In your final hotel fight, defend against flanking enemies from all sides.

All that remains is to follow the map to the remote detonator in the room up ahead on your right. You can be proud. You've beaten the odds and stopped a catastrophic bomb from going off *twice*.

Shut down the remote detonator with a minute to spare.

MISSION 14: AIRPORT

Only one loose end remains: Juan Crespo. On your last mission—a solo journey—you are to make sure Crespo never tries another stunt like the one in New Orleans. In other words, Crespo had better fill out his last will and testament. First, though, you'll have to evade his airport security staff while planting a bomb and fight through a terrorist army to get your hands on Crespo. Even then, you won't have a chance to catch him, but do you need to?

You begin with the M16A2 cocked and ready, but you can't fire a single shot during the first part of your stealth mission.

Guns & Ammo

Time to play with the best toys again. The M16A2, along with the G3A3, is the game's best assault rifle. Scores of 39 range, 66 damage, and 74 accuracy put it tops in its class, and its 30-round clips put it over the top.

Stocked with ammo and a nice kick, the M16A2 will prove valuable on the mission—when you get the green light to fire it.

On the backup front, it's the debut of the SR-2. Rather than go with the traditional M203 grenade launcher in this spot, we're talking a submachine gun. Better to be safe and take the extra firepower; you're on a solo mission and can't ask others to do your shooting for you. The two grenade slots carry the M34 and the standard frag. No hostages in this one.

If one guard sees you inside the airport, the mission fails right then and there.

Shadow Games

From the starting room, exit through the door hidden in darkness. It leads to a long corridor patrolled by a single guard.

You have two choices to start your stealth mission into the airport.

The correct choice lies to your left: the door hidden in darkness. Open the door and peek out until you spot the guard on his patrol down the corridor. Sit patient until the guard disappears from sight and then run down the corridor and find the stairs on the right side.

Walk upstairs and wait for the guard in the hallway to leave.

Walk slowly up the stairs. Noise from this point on could give you away. At the top of the stairs, do not turn the corner to your right until you're sure it's safe. The guard patrols almost to the stairs, but not quite, so you can wait him out. Watch the glass wall for his shadow, and when it disappears and you hear the footsteps recede, turn the corner.

Walk to the door and wait there until you hear the door in the next room open and close. The guard has continued his patrol and passed through to the following room. Open the door and walk straight across the kitchen to the door that leads to the outside deck.

Without a shot fired, you're outside with only a single guard to go.

Now only a single guard stands between you and your objective. From the deck's corner, search for the guard in the parking lot below. Click over to night vision if you have to and scan the shadows. The guard walks in a vaguely circular pattern around the parking lot perimeter. You can use the truck and the van parked in the middle as shields. So long as you keep him on the opposite side at all times, you can venture to any parking lot spot.

Reach the third vehicle without being seen.

When he starts his route behind the truck, slide down the ladder and hightail it over to the truck's nearside. Peek out from the truck's rear and wait till the guard begins his walk back toward the deck before you start to move toward the third vehicle.

With the tan van and truck between you and the clueless guard, you should be able to cross to the red van in plenty of time. Do your thing and Crespo will never know you've set a grand trap for him.

Plant your explosives in the van and you can flick off the safety lock on your M16.

Chasing Crespo

Cap the parking lot guard and the one inside on the way to the hangar.

Finally, after you trigger the first objective, you can start triggering your gun. The secrecy ban is over and—look out!—it's time to wreak some major havoc. As a start, target the parking lot guard and let him have it.

Scan the area behind the truck (to the right of the deck) for stairs going up to a back door. Follow the hall to the hangar office. Along the way, you'll meet one patrolling guard. Since you've been in the stealth mode so long, it shouldn't be a stretch to sneak up on him and drop him without anyone, including the poor guard, the wiser.

Nuke the rocket launcher first, then track down the surrounding guards.

Go cautious before you hit the airport tarmac. As soon as you enter the office before the tarmac, the rocket-launcher guard on the other side will shoot a missile into the room. Just step too close to the door and you should be fine. After the blast, step out through the door and blast the two guards hiding in the crates to your left (one of these will be the rocket launcher). Then aim straight ahead and take down the two guards past the airplane. Though you've taken four guards down in three seconds, this alerts the other guards who switch into a full-court press.

From the cover of the first plane, wipe out all enemies looking to head you off.

Bounce up to the airplane and start picking off guys as they try to flank you on your left side. Fortunately, the hangar lies to your right, so they can't come from that direction. You will be able to nail two to three terrorists, before you have to duck behind the plane and reload.

When you've got the terrorists settled into a defensive posture, zoom in on the front of the hangar. Two guards protect the front entrance, one to the right of the corner and one to the left. Blast the terrorist closest to you, then worry about any terrorist sneaking up at the corner.

Pick off the lone guard in front of the hangar.

Before you commit to the garage area, stay put for a minute and see if any more terrorists show up out on the tarmac.

You're almost ready to make your assault on the hangar interior, but give it a few more seconds. Some stragglers may show up late for the party. If they do, welcome them with an invitation to the afterlife. The second you start across the tarmac's open space, a second rocket-launcher terrorist will assault you from your left. Look for him out past the gate by the two planes in the distance. He will try to run up close and shoot a missile into your midsection. Don't let him.

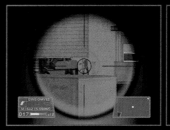 

Try to pick off the two guards inside the garage at long range.

Next, move up to the crates in front of the garage area. A short distance ahead the garage looms large. Even though the garage door is cracked only half open, you can still scope out the two guards inside, one to either side of the forklift. Snipe them from the safety of your outside position.

Battle it out with the third guard in the garage to make the last checkpoint.

The third garage guard can prove troublesome, however. You must enter the garage to get a shot off at him, and yet he's up on the balcony aiming down on you—a much better shot. You'll have to do some hit-and-run tactics. Dart into the garage and trigger a short barrage up at him, then dart back outside. The guard will return fire and most—and hopefully, all—damage will ricochet off the top section of the garage door. Repeat until you knock him off his perch.

Bon Voyage

You have to force Crespo toward his compromised plane, and what better way than with a grenade?

Don't get overzealous here. Too much enthusiasm and you'll end up killing Crespo inside the hangar, when all you're supposed to do is scare him. You see, you want his death to look like an accident, so you must drive him toward his plane and the plastic explosive present you've left him.

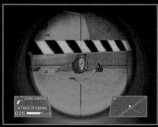

Look left first as you enter Crespo's hangar.

The best approach? Lob a "warning" grenade into Crespo's section of the garage. Throw it into the far corner and you should send him running. You may get lucky and kill a few of his men too.

The guards in the middle will prove hardest to hit because of the obstacles you're forced to shoot around.

After the grenade goes off, work your way toward the front of the nearby Dumpster. This protects you from almost any attack if you stay crouched behind it. Look left first and clip the guard up on the balcony, who might have the best chance to hit you. Drill anyone you see moving around the vans.

From the van, you can beat the rest of the hangar guards.

Now slide to the Dumpster's right side and see if you can find anyone to target. Continue out, laying down cover fire, as you make for the van to your right. The middle guards are the hardest to hit, since so many obstacles are in the way. From the van, though, you should have the angle on anyone. If not, give them time and they'll break from cover and you can pick them off then. Every once in a while, take a peek at the van's rear so no one sneaks up on you.

Challenge the next guard, but beware of the incoming rocket.

Give it some time and you'll clear the hangar. When you can run freely across the garage, visit the door on the opposite-side wall. This will eventually lead you to a room with a long window along the left side overlooking another section of garage below. Across the room, through an open doorway, a single guard will challenge you. If he's not in firing range, he'll be hiding around the corner, so don't forget about him after you clear the room.

From the bombed room, shoot down on the terrorists waiting below.

Open up on the guard, but don't advance too far into the room. As soon as you step foot in there, the two guards in the garage below launch grenades through the window and it's an instant inferno. You'll be a cooked goose if you linger. Instead, drop back after killing the guard (or stepping into the room) and bunker down in the previous room. The explosion will go off without much more than a slight burn for you.

Tip

Chase Crespo to his plane, but not at the expense of being careless while battling his henchmen.

Time for a little payback. From the window the grenades just zipped through, you have excellent shots down on the terrorist guards. They won't think they're so hot anymore as you have the upper hand in the combat this time. Fire a couple of bursts at each one, and don't leave until you see slumped bodies on the ground.

Surprise the first three guards out by the runway.

The last door leads out onto the tarmac again. You have a fuel truck parked directly in front of you, and three terrorists flank it in a triangular position to stop you once and for all.

From the doorway, target the left terrorist, since you both have clear shots at each other. Don't spare any ammo now; you're almost finished and won't get a second crack at Crespo's elite bodyguards...unless you feel like starting all over again.

Next, pick off the middle terrorist who will probably use the back end of the truck as protection. While you assault him, the third terrorist tries to flank you on the right side. Deal with the second terrorist as quickly as you can so you have time to adjust to the third's tactics.

As Crespo's plane takes off on its disastrous last flight, gun down the final two terrorists and hang up your boots.

You'll hear the whine of Crespo's jet as it begins takeoff. That sound spells doom for Crespo; a few minutes from now and he'll be in itty-bitty pieces. All that remains are two guards out by the runway. No real worries, as you have no reason to rush and can set up perfect shots if you like.

Believe it or not, you've just beaten the game. It's been a long road, full of mystery, suspense and more action than a suicidal Hollywood stuntman gets in a career. Of course, you wouldn't have it any other way.

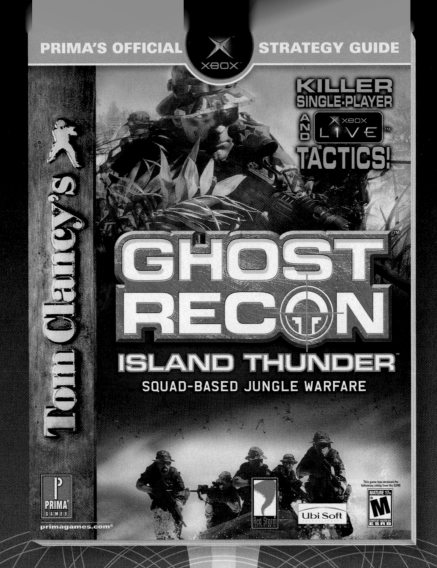